▲

"In *Shifting the Balance*, Kari and Jan have masterfully dispelled many of the myths and misunderstandings associated with reading instruction. Additionally, they offer classroom teachers and coaches six simple, practical shifts that have the power to transform the way we teach children how to read. Indeed, balanced literacy and science do exist in harmony, and we practitioners can offer our children both concurrently. Thank you, Kari and Jan, for this important work that is sure to change lives!"

—Christina Nosek, co-author of *To Know and Nurture a Reader:*
Conferring with Confidence and Joy

▲

"*In Shifting the Balance*, Jan Burkins and Kari Yates provide a safe space for teachers to courageously examine some long-held balanced literacy practices and turn a critical eye to where those practices have gotten out of balance. If you're willing to be vulnerable and move towards resolving the gap between research and practice, this book provides actionable steps you can take to shift your thinking and bring instruction into alignment with the scientific evidence."

—Helen White, Instructional Support Teacher, Northside Independent School District

▲

"Burkins and Yates are intent on building a bridge in *Shifting the Balance* by finding compelling opportunities in K–2 classrooms to align research and instructional practice. One of the several issues they discuss is intentionally supporting oral language development in the classroom, a key aspect of literacy instruction that is missing or misunderstood regardless of approach. They find common ground and build a broader understanding that leads to a strong comprehensive literacy design."

—Adria Klein, Professor Emeritus, CSU San Bernardino

"What are the research-based, critical elements for teaching reading? In *Shifting the Balance*, Jan and Kari give you the information, classroom examples, and tools to help you make the best decisions around six key shifts for instruction. After reviewing the misunderstandings, the science, and the needs of your students, you will be able to audit your current practices (individually, in a PLC, or system-wide) to provide responsive and effective literacy learning for all your students."

> —Fran McVeigh, Teacher, Consultant, #G2Great Chat Moderator
> and Associate Academic Coordinator for Morningside College

"In *Shifting the Balance*, Jan and Kari invite us to reflect and reexamine our beliefs about teaching reading. They gently nudge us to rethink and possibly adjust our early literacy practices. Jan and Kari have taken on this controversial topic by embracing vulnerability and modeling what it means to be truly reflective practitioners. This book is a must read for new *and* veteran teachers!"

> — Jennifer Allen, Literacy Specialist, Waterville Public Schools, ME

"*Shifting the Balance* is a welcoming opportunity to reexamine our familiar teaching practices. Without *judgment*, Burkins and Yates invigorate these practices by inviting educators to make scientific shifts in the systems that have been in place for years. This book will revolutionize reading instruction and in turn, the lives of countless students."

> —Jennifer Clyne Stewart, M.Ed., Dyslexia Specialist

"This book speaks to teachers. It is overwhelmingly clear that Jan Burkins and Kari Yates have been and are immersed in the world of today's classrooms. *Shifting the Balance* will help many rethink instruction in ways that will support all students. In the current version of the Reading Wars, it is difficult for any of us to say we were wrong about some of our beliefs or practices. And thus, few do. However, Jan Burkins and Kari Yates have done just that. This is as commendable as it is unusual."

> –David Liben, www.readingdoneright.org

"Science of Reading, Balanced Literacy, Reading Wars—what is a school to do? Who do we listen to? The six shifts introduced in *Shifting the Balance* became our launching point for our campus, resulting in a solid foundation for our reading instruction that allows us to develop joyful, strong readers who love books, love to read, and are equipped to successfully navigate the print and make meaning while doing so. Don't just read this book: debate, discuss, and learn from Jan and Kari's ideas and impact your children just like we are!"

—Kristy Thomas, Principal of Rock Rest Elementary

"Finally, a book that has the power to stop the literacy pendulum swings! In *Shifting the Balance*, Burkins and Yates skillfully explore 'balanced literacy' and 'the science of reading' to find the sweet spots where they overlap, connect, and actually complement one another. The result is a resource that raises our level of instruction while helping children discover and reap the joyful rewards of reading."

—Susie Rolander, Bank Street College

"This book found me at just the right time! *Shifting the Balance* gives voice to the questions I've had in my mind about Balanced Literacy and the Science of Reading and provides clear insights on how to connect the best parts of both to benefit early readers. Throughout the book, Jan and Kari confirm practices worth holding onto while providing actionable next steps I can't wait to implement with students to strengthen my reading instruction."

—Kristen Mullikin, Reading Specialist, Elk Grove Unified School District

SHIFTING

THE

BALANCE

6 Ways to Bring the Science of Reading
into the Balanced Literacy Classroom

n Burkins

Kari Yates

Stenhouse
PUBLISHERS

www.stenhouse.com

PORTSMOUTH, NEW HAMPSHIRE

www.stenhouse.com

Copyright © 2021 by Jan Burkins and Kari Yates

Library of Congress Cataloging-in-Publication Data

Names: Burkins, Jan Miller, author. | Yates, Kari, author.
Title: Shifting the balance : 6 ways to bring the science of reading into
   the balanced literacy classroom / Jan Burkins and Kari Yates.
Description: Portsmouth, New Hampshire : Stenhouse Publishers, [2021] |
   Includes bibliographical references and index. |
Identifiers: LCCN 2020034486 (print) | LCCN 2020034487 (ebook) | ISBN
   9781625315106 (paperback) | ISBN 9781625315113 (ebook)
Subjects: LCSH: Reading (Early childhood) | Reading comprehension—Study
   and teaching (Early childhood) | Reading—Phonetic method—Study and
   teaching (Early childhood)
Classification: LCC LB1139.5.R43 B87 2021 (print) | LCC LB1139.5.R43
   (ebook) | DDC 372.4—dc23
LC record available at https://lccn.loc.gov/2020034486
LC ebook record available at https://lccn.loc.gov/2020034487

Cover design: Cindy Butler
Interior design, and typesetting by Gina Poirier

Manufactured in the United States of America

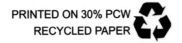

PRINTED ON 30% PCW
RECYCLED PAPER

26 25 25 24 23 22 21   9 8 7 6 5 4 3 2

For curious and courageous teachers everywhere,
who daily stretch themselves on behalf of children.

—Jan and Kari

CONTENTS

▼ ▼ ▼ ▼ ▼ ▼ ▼

ACKNOWLEDGMENTS

More Than a Little Bit

We agree. This is the hardest writing work either of us has ever done. So we arrive at the end of this project a little bit weary, yet more than a little bit grateful.

To our husbands, you are more than a little bit alike in your fiercely loving ways. Thank you for insisting that we eat and sleep, and even have some fun, when we got more than a little bit preoccupied with this project. You know how to hold us close *and* turn us loose, so that we can put energy into work that brings us joy. We love you.

To our beloved children and grandchildren, you have been more than a little bit patient with our split attention. We hope we have modeled the power of finding a passion to relentlessly pursue, and that you know our hearts are yours entirely and without condition.

To our loving parents, our wise mentors, our dear friends, and our coauthors on previous books, you have shaped our lives and helped us grow into who we are. We are more than a little bit grateful for the ways each of you have taught and nurtured us along the way.

To our whole Stenhouse family, who took a little bit of a risk with this project, thank you for believing in this book, and in us. We are deeply grateful to Amanda Bondi, whose leadership, creativity, and patience transformed the raw materials of this manuscript into the beautifully designed text you hold in your hands. And finally, to our extraordinary editor, Terry Thompson, who is endlessly wise and kind and funny. Without your vision and smarts, this book wouldn't be a book at all. We are more than a little bit honored to have had you work alongside us.

Finally, we are grateful to the teachers, instructional coaches, principals, and district leaders with whom we work. You are more than a little bit committed to doing what is right for children, even when it is more than a little bit uncomfortable. You give us a whole lot of hope for this world.

INTRODUCTION

Embracing Science *and* Balance

I f you're in there with the kids every day, doing your level best to help five-, six-, and seven-year-olds learn how to connect squiggly little marks on a page to meaningful ideas, it would be easy to feel attacked or confused by the rhetoric about beginning reading instruction.

From talk radio to blogs to the evening news to state legislatures, everywhere we turn these days, someone seems to be voicing an opinion about reading instruction in schools.

Some argue that there is a disconnect between research and classroom practice. Some argue that things are out of balance in the balanced literacy classroom. Still others argue that the methods in many classrooms are making learning to read harder rather than easier, especially for the children most at risk of reading difficulties.

The public debate is rooted in widespread concern that too many children aren't learning to read as well as they need to. Of course it's easy to take issue with standardized assessments or to question exactly what various numbers mean.

But can we really argue with the fact that, despite our current and best efforts, many children are still having a lot of trouble learning to read?

Chances are there are children experiencing reading difficulties in your own school as well. And probably, if your data are reflective of the historic and national trends, a disproportionate number of the children having reading difficulties are children of color and/or are from marginalized communities (Morgan et al. 2017; Hanford 2020; Rearden et al. 2018). Perhaps these are the very reasons you picked up this book.

1

Many educators—whether "balanced literacy" or "science of reading" proponents—are gravely concerned and committed to disrupting systems that perpetuate reading failure. Many science of reading advocates blame balanced literacy for inequitable literacy outcomes. And many balanced literacy advocates resist the science of reading fearing it will make literacy access even *more* inequitable. We would argue that this dichotomy is false and neither side's concerns should be dismissed.

All children, especially those locked into systems that seem to guarantee their failure (Minor 2018), need access to both the secrets of the alphabetic code *and* relevant experiences with texts. They need both explicit information about how reading works *and* immersive experiences that show them how to leverage reading and writing to change the world.

In truth, most science of reading proponents actually *do* want children to have great books and time to read them, and most balanced literacy educators *do* want children to know how the phonetic system works. We hope this book will help you make space—both in your head and in your heart—to give *all* children access to all the tools and experiences they need to live literate lives and to become agents of change.

If you are a school leader, chances are, you are sifting through the politics and the pressure, the research and the needs of all the children in your building to arrive at some kernel of instructional truth. Finding answers is time-consuming at best, a moving target at worst. For example, as the response to Emily Hanford's "Hard Words" article (2018) rippled across the country, a relentlessly reflective principal who we deeply respect asked us point blank, "What are you going to do to help us figure this out?"

Not long after, we had an inquiry from a frustrated literacy coach who had been told by district leadership she could no longer use the MSV model in workshops with teachers. Interactions like these, together with our own cognitive dissonance, sealed our commitment to building a bridge between the science of reading and balanced literacy.

Our work is driven by a fierce commitment to you—the real champions of education—who work closely with children every day. We've written this book to support you in making sound decisions anchored in the best of science, the truth of responsiveness, and a relentless focus on providing all children learning experiences saturated with meaning.

Bravely Embracing Research and Balance

In response to the growing division and rising intensity around early literacy instruction, we've mustered our courage and chosen to embrace the national conversation as an opportunity to sort through the noise, in search of the signal of sound practice.

With our shared interest in early literacy piqued by those who suggest that balanced literacy practices don't represent scientific findings about reading instruction, we have taken a systematic and deep look at experimental research. This work required us to honestly consider evidence and arguments that challenged some of our most closely held beliefs. It meant pushing ourselves to read beyond the sensationalized and often misleading media headlines. It meant reading through reams of research summaries and meta-analyses, as well as books and articles and blogs, written by teachers, professors of education, the federal government, educational psychologists, and neuroscientists. And most importantly, it meant intentionally initiating conversations with those who take issue with some of the ideas we hold most dear. We have tried to do this work with our minds open enough—and our limbic systems calm enough—to learn as much as possible along the way.

Through it all we found, as have others, that the experimental research on reading isn't completely consistent or irrefutable. Furthermore, research is even less clear or consistent when it comes to the nitty-gritty nuances of classroom instruction, such as the exact order for introducing letters and sounds. However, the experimental science that establishes how the brain learns to read *is* far too comprehensive and too robust to disregard.

Immersing ourselves in this controversial topic was often vulnerable work. Sometimes we found ourselves triggered or defensive, fiercely scribbling responses in the margins of our texts and wanting to argue, "That's a misrepresentation! That's a partial truth. They don't understand!" Other times we found ourselves excitedly jotting notes that showed the strong connectedness of ideas that could bring the two sides together rather than push us apart.

Along the way we have asked ourselves:

▲ Is it possible that balanced literacy classrooms *are* sometimes a bit out of balance when it comes to understanding and promoting research-aligned instruction?

▲ Could it be that we *are* missing (or misunderstanding) compelling opportunities to bridge research to instructional practice in the reading classroom?

▲ Do we have some seemingly logical practices that *are* driven more by our intuition about how reading appears to work from the *outside* than they are driven by the science of how reading actually works *inside* the brain?

▲ Is it possible that a few simple but powerful shifts *could* help us unlock literacy for more children than ever before, especially those for whom the current systems do not work, or do not work well enough?

We have found that the answer to all four of these questions is *yes*.

One thing that has become crystal clear to us is that the very term *balanced literacy* triggers a negative response from some people whose voices we need to hear and learn from. In the minds of some, balanced literacy is simply "whole language" repackaged with a different name. Others view it as a haphazard approach designed to appease critics by simply doing "a bit of everything." Still others criticize balanced literacy for tokenism, giving only a small, symbolic nod to experimental science and calling that enough (Brady 2020). Although we don't ascribe to these descriptions as a rule, we do agree that a common definition of balanced literacy is difficult to pin down and that balanced literacy plays out differently from school to school and classroom to classroom.

Yet, despite some imperfections of balanced literacy in theory and some inconsistencies in practice, we hold tight to the promise of the term *balance* and how it so beautifully defines the complex and informed equilibrium classroom teachers *must* constantly pursue in a field brimming with competing tensions.

Having chosen this journey, our ideas have evolved. We are balanced literacy advocates who have studied the perspective of "the other side" and have returned home, no longer frustrated, upset, or feeling like picking a fight. Instead we've come back with fresh eyes and ears, with insights and information. We've come back home better understanding gaps and overlaps. Most importantly, we've come back inspired with a new sense of possibility and purpose because we now know there *are* shifts we can embrace to help *more children* learn to read and *with less struggle*.

The good news? The shifts we need to make are not big shifts! They may take courage, but they are manageable, yet powerful changes that you can make without sacrificing the heart of balanced literacy.

How We've Organized This Book

And so, we offer the book you hold in your hands as a pathway forward to more robust instruction for beginning readers, starting with six simple and scientifically sound shifts. The six shifts we offer—although each tackling a distinct and important idea of its own—connect to and build on each other, making their collective impact even more promising. Our greatest hope is that being thoughtful about how we bring more of the experimental science of teaching reading into the balanced literacy classroom will give you both clarity and energy and ultimately result in brighter outcomes for children.

The science you will learn in this book is also cumulative, with each shift building on the ideas of those before it. Each chapter, or shift, also focuses on revising a practice that—as logical as it may seem—turns out to be based more on intuition than on what children really need to become proficient readers. If you've been watching the current literacy debate, you may be asking some of these questions already:

- ▲ But isn't reading all about meaning making?
- ▲ What is the big deal about phonemic awareness, anyway?
- ▲ Where's the fun in phonics?
- ▲ Don't kids just have to memorize sight words?
- ▲ Isn't English too unreliable to teach children to "sound it out"?
- ▲ Aren't decodable texts loaded with problems?

We'll explore some answers to these questions, and much more, in the coming pages. Because we've packed a whole lot of information into this book, it is designed for easy navigation. Along with color-coding the shifts, we've also organized each of the chapters around a common structure made up of the following six consistent sections.

1. A Look Inside a Classroom

At the beginning of each shift, we step inside a classroom where a familiar early literacy practice is being enacted with the very best of intentions. These are practices you may recognize. Although they may make sense on an intuitive level—or what Marilyn Adams describes as "from the outside in"—they need to be revisited (1990).

2. Clearing Up Some Confusion

Here, we take a look at some common misunderstandings that drive current practices and offer a summary of some of the important science to consider as we rethink and revise our mental models for instructional decision making.

3. A Short Summary of the Science

Each shift's discussion of the misunderstandings is followed by a bulleted list that succinctly summarizes the science within the shift.

4. Recommendations for Making the Shift

We open this section with a quick-reference list of high-leverage routines and then zoom in on some of them. We include simple and scientifically sound changes that all educators can make to their practice, weaving this science through balanced literacy's instructional contexts—read-aloud, shared reading, guided reading, independent reading, writing, and word work.

5. Meanwhile, Back in the Classroom . . .

In this section, we revisit the classroom that opened the chapter to see how the teacher has elevated literacy practices by considering the related reading science and making a few key, intentional changes.

6. Questions for Reflection

Finally, we follow each shift with reflective questions to guide your own thoughtful planning and decision making, as you work to choose next steps for the students you serve.

To fit in all the science and instructional recommendations we wanted to include, without the book getting too long, we decided to house many of the resources at our website, **TheSixShifts.com.** Throughout the book, we direct you to the site, where you can download resources, assessments, and more in-depth tools. For starters, you may want to go there to download our "Teacher-Friendly Guide to Making Sense of Scientific Research," which will give some insight into the way we approached the research that supports this book.

Finding Grace and Learning from Each Other

The work we invite you into *is not* purely academic or technical in nature. It can also be emotionally taxing work, especially when it calls on us to reevaluate long-held beliefs or practices.

As you commit to take an honest, second look at the balanced literacy practices in your system, school, or classroom—in order to spot misunderstandings, misinformation, and missed opportunities—we hope you will also find grace for yourself. To that end, we share with you the commitments we crafted for ourselves as we stepped into this vulnerable work.

We commit to . . .

- ▲ Being kind to ourselves, making peace with the unavoidable reality that *there are things* we have missed, misunderstood, and misinterpreted

- ▲ Honestly appraising our current practices with an open heart and open mind

- ▲ Recognizing and reflecting on our own triggers and biases

- ▲ Actively working to lower our defenses so we can raise our awareness

- ▲ Reconsidering, reprioritizing, or simply letting go of less helpful practices, to make space for some that are more effective

- ▲ Taking action rather than giving in to the paralysis of self-doubt and/or overwhelm

As classroom teachers and school leaders, we invite you to let this text serve as a bridge from argument to action, from misunderstanding to movement, from confusion to clarity, and from polarization to practicality.

Time is precious. Let's begin.

RETHINKING HOW READING COMPREHENSION BEGINS

It's Monday morning, and as his second graders enter the building from the playground, Mr. Tucker stands poised at the classroom door. Amid the chorus of early morning chatter at Lakeside Elementary School, Mr. Tucker greets the children warmly, offering hugs, high fives, and home language "Hellos" for his multilingual students. A few students stop to chat with him, and Mr. Tucker nods, smiles, and then nudges them forward to begin their daily routines.

On the other side of the door, students begin the morning routines they know well. They mark their lunch choices and make their way to their seats. Next, they pull out self-selected independent reading texts and begin reading silently, while Mr. Tucker takes care of some housekeeping. When he is finished, he calls the children to the gathering space for read-aloud.

Today the children are excited to hear more about Frog and Toad's antics. He knows his students have come to love these characters and their adventures and that everyone can easily understand these texts, even his students who are still quite new to English.

At the conclusion of the read-aloud, Mr. Tucker asks the children to talk with a partner. As he listens in about the character traits they noticed in today's adventure, he hears many of his students offer short—even one-word—answers with descriptors like *funny, mad, sad, nice.* When he hears a few students use more sophisticated vocabulary, like *frustrated, thoughtful,* and *concerned,* he finds himself reflecting on the vast differences in vocabulary among his diverse class of learners.

Next, Mr. Tucker reviews the day's literacy choice menu, work that students will do independently while he meets with small groups at the guided reading table. Today's options include independent reading, writing about reading, choosing an audible book at the computer station, or sorting a list of words with the week's spelling pattern, *-igh*. The children quietly move to get their materials and begin working. Mr. Tucker expresses his appreciation for their silent transition. Next, he gathers his first small group for instruction.

Today's text is an L level text called "Rocks and Minerals." He was excited to find this text in the guided reading library after seeing how fascinated all the kids seemed with the extensive rock collection Ramon had shared with the class on Friday.

Ramon, with all of his background knowledge, is eager to dig in, reading with confidence, studying pictures, and excitedly making comments to his classmates as he reads, *"Igneous* means fire" and "Oh, yeah. Sedimentary rocks are cool because you can sort of break them apart with your hands, like Superman."

But despite a more supportive book introduction, Mr. Tucker is surprised by how hard today's text seems for several of the other children.

Kenesha labors to chunk out several longer words, but she simply doesn't have the background knowledge she needs to make sense of their meaning.

Olivia, on the other hand, seems to breeze through the words on the first few pages, sounding accurate and fluent when she reads aloud, but when Mr. Tucker asks her, "So, what are you learning about rocks so far?" She looks a bit panicked and says, "They are under the ground?"

It seems to him that every year he has students with similar profiles. They have made adequate progress in kindergarten and first grade. They've moved with relative ease through the emergent and early stages of reading development. But now, as they move into books with more complex content and vocabulary, their comprehension seems to drop off, despite decoding many individual words with relative ease.

A COMMON PRACTICE TO RECONSIDER

▲ ▼ ▼ ▼ ▼ ▼

Overlooking the role of listening comprehension in reading comprehension.

Quite clearly, Mr. Tucker cares deeply about his students. He values read-aloud, small-group instruction, and students' independent explorations of books. Mr. Tucker is respectful and responsive toward his students.

For many of us, our work in classrooms has looked similar. We have done the tricky dance of balancing time, efficiency, engagement, classroom noise levels, standards-based instruction, and student learning. But in many cases our students have needed more opportunities to engage in rich and expansive conversation with us and with each other. And, despite the best of intentions, some of our instructional choices may be placing a ceiling on students' thinking and vocabulary development, which will eventually limit their reading comprehension.

Meanwhile, we work hard to teach comprehension via strategy instruction, often overlooking the quintessential prerequisite that children must understand enough of the language structures and vocabulary that make up what they *hear*. Listening comprehension—which is built through language interaction—is, after all, an essential precondition of reading comprehension (Catts, Adlof, and Ellis-Weismer 2006; Gough and Tunmer 1986; Hoover and Gough 1990; Nation et al. 2010; Lervåg, Hulme, and Melby-Lervåg 2017).

By *listening comprehension*, we are not referring to how well children follow directions or to how well they can sit for us to offer long explanations. We are referring, instead, to their capacity to understand spoken language. This capacity develops through conversation, through hearing and sharing personal stories, and through interactions with rich texts. All of this exposes children to new ideas, new language structures, new vocabulary, and new concepts, until they can access these for themselves by reading increasingly complex texts.

Clearing Up Some Confusion

Comprehension is the true goal of any encounter with print. In fact, sense-making *is* the point of print, so it's critical that we understand some important things about how the ability to comprehend develops. Let's dig a little deeper and explore a few common misunderstandings about reading comprehension, along with some reading science that clarifies them.

MISUNDERSTANDING:

Reading comprehension begins with print.

To think about what it takes to comprehend a text and what it really means to read, consider the following paragraph:

> *El aubelo dormia en el sofá de la sala y los ronquidos le salían entre los dientes. Sus pies eran gordos y masuados como tameles gruesos y se los polveaba y los metia en calcetines blancos y zapatos de cuero café. (Cisneros 1994)*

Although both of us have enough rudimentary Spanish to decode pretty much every word in this paragraph with appropriate emphasis and mostly accurate pronunciation, we cannot actually understand it beyond a few seemingly unrelated words—*dientes* (teeth), *zapatas* (shoes), *café* (coffee). So, when we "read" this passage, either aloud or in our minds, our listening brain doesn't comprehend it, because we don't actually know Spanish as a spoken language.

This illustration shows how reading comprehension works. To comprehend a text, enough words on the page have to activate language we already have in our heads.

Intuitively, it may seem that children don't begin the work of reading comprehension until they start learning to read. Although this makes logical sense, it is not the truth of what goes on inside the brain as children learn to make sense of text. Reading comprehension actually begins long before children begin to decode. It begins as they learn to understand and use spoken language (Hogan, Adlof, and Alonzo 2014).

Let us explain.

In the brain, the work of comprehending spoken language, or listening comprehension, involves three different processing systems, or networks, that are connected by neural pathways (Adams 1990; Berninger and Richards 2002;

Dehaene 2013; Seidenberg and McClelland 1989; Seidenberg 2013, 2017). These systems are illustrated in Figure 1.1.

▲ The *phonological processing system* listens for and produces speech sounds. It also gathers chunks of meaning from a stream of spoken language, which activates the meaning processing system.

▲ Once activated, the *meaning processing system* retrieves every meaning that the listener has stored for the word. It also collects and organizes word meanings for retrieval later.

▲ The *context processing system* works with the meaning processing system to use background knowledge, putting words into a larger context to decide which meaning fits the context.

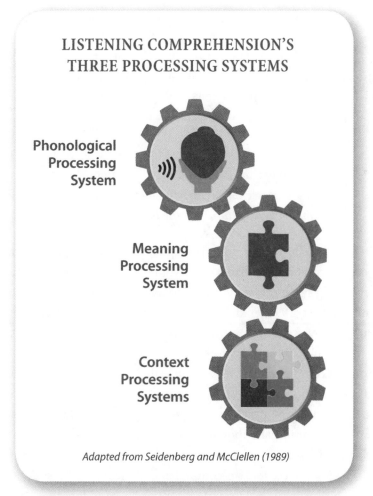

LISTENING COMPREHENSION'S
THREE PROCESSING SYSTEMS

Phonological
Processing
System

Meaning
Processing
System

Context
Processing
Systems

Adapted from Seidenberg and McClellen (1989)

FIGURE 1.1 Listening Comprehension's Three Processing Systems

These three processing systems are built into the wiring of the human brain; they are part of the genetically organized hardware we are born with (Adams 1990; Seidenberg and McClellen 1989; Seidenberg 2017). The systems develop and grow "naturally" as children hear language models, interact with those around them, and get feedback on their language attempts. The more spoken language children process and store through this system—learning language syntax, developing vocabulary, building background knowledge, and more—the more developed their neuronal structures will be and the stronger their listening comprehension will become (Cervetti et. al 2020; Kintsch and Kintsch 2005).

It might seem obvious that listening comprehension can break down when we hear new and unknown words, as you would probably experience upon hearing this sentence:

The child was clearly panivorous.

But even when we *do* know all the words, it's still possible to struggle with listening comprehension, because it requires that we weave together many ideas (Kintsch and Kintsch 2005).

Imagine hearing this bit of a story:

We tried to get rid of the squirrel, but he loved it too much. Even though the squirrel was still around, the rabbit began to show up regularly. And the duck, with its incessant noise, seemed to always be about the house.

Even though you understood every word of this passage (meaning processing system), you probably had to shift your thinking with each sentence (context processing system) as you worked to make sense of the text (Graesser, Singer, and Trabasso 1994; Seidenberg 2017). And, as we introduce the title, "The Puppy's Toys," your thinking is likely shifting again.

Let's look a bit more closely at the three processing systems, which make listening comprehension possible, in action. In a recent conversation, Kari said to Jan, "Cards are really important to my husband." Table 1.1 describes the work of each processing system as Jan's listening brain tried to make sense of what Kari said. Jan initially thought that Kari was referring to playing cards. But when Kari finally inserted the word *birthday* into the speech stream, everything clicked into place, and Jan comprehended that buying just the right card for Kari's birthday is really important for her husband John.

TABLE 1.1

THE LANGUAGE PROCESSING SYSTEMS IN ACTION

The System and What It Does	How It Processes Each Word
Phonological processing systems	**Hears and recognizes** the word *cards* in the sentence "Cards are really important to my husband. . . . ," and **activates** the meaning processing system.
Meaning processing system	**Reviews** stored vocabulary for possible meanings for the word *cards*: • playing cards • greeting cards • Social Security cards • index cards • recipe cards • credit cards
Context processing system	**Considers** the surrounding context, background knowledge, and language structure to **choose** the appropriate meaning and form a hypothesis: *She and her husband like to play cards.* When meaning is disrupted—"He never wants our kids to get a birthday gift without the perfect card"—it **prompts** the meaning processing system to reevaluate.

This table is, of course, an oversimplification of the process. All of the complex back and forth of the processing systems messaging each other and working together, all while more words continue to flow into the language systems, happens at faster than lightning speed. In fact, listening comprehension happens at a speed that makes lightning look like molasses (Dahaene 2009; Seidenberg 2017).

Again, given exposure and practice, all of this listening comprehension work comes relatively easily to us . . . the work of listening for meaning, of retrieving vocabulary, of using context, of connecting ideas, and of monitoring for sense-making. We have literally been learning how to understand spoken language from the moment we were born (Hogan, Adlof, and Alonzo 2014; DeCasper and Spence 1986). And all of this second-nature listening comprehension, which evolved through language interactions (Wolf 2007), comes full circle when we eventually use this same language to comprehend what we read.

MISUNDERSTANDING:

Understanding spoken language and understanding written language are two different things.

Now that you understand the brain's mechanisms for listening comprehension, we are excited to tell you a really important secret. Reading comprehension is fundamentally the same work as listening comprehension. That is, reading comprehension and spoken language comprehension share the same three language processing systems—phonological, context, and meaning.

Quite simply (and not so simply), print is spoken language written down (Dehaene 2009; Wolf 2007). As reading teachers, this connection may not be something we typically think about, and the subtlety may seem a bit like a fine distinction (or even irrelevant) to reading comprehension. But this connection is actually a potent and critical one for understanding how reading comprehension works.

Here's the thing . . .

Written language was invented so that we could take the words we say—which would otherwise disappear into the air—and pin them down on the page for retrieval later (Wolf 2007). Once retrieved, they are reconstituted back into spoken language. Then they are *heard* and understood, via the language processing systems introduced in Figure 1.1.

Reading comprehension actually involves translating the words on the page into spoken language and "listening to them," either by saying them aloud or saying them in our heads. Seidenberg (2017) explains that, as children read and articulate the words represented by the written text, the words are "comprehended by the spoken-language system, establishing the necessary bridge between print and speech" (119). This means that silent reading isn't really silent! By "hearing" the words, the brain's spoken language processing mechanism can now do the work of listening to them and comprehending them (listening comprehension). This listening to spoken language, whether aloud or "internal phonological codes," happens every time we read and comprehend text (Seidenberg 2017).

For example, you didn't simply *read* the words in the last paragraph, you actually said them "aloud" in your head. By turning the written words into spoken language again, even though the speech was in your mind, it allowed your phonological, meaning, and context processing systems to "hear" and comprehend them, as they do all spoken language.

So, if children cannot understand enough of the words and sentences when they are spoken, they will not comprehend the same words and sentences when they read them.

This means that opportunities to grow *oral language*—including vocabulary, background knowledge, sentence structure, and more—actually develop the comprehension mechanisms of *reading* (Quinn et al. 2015; Lervåg, Hulme, and Melby-Lervåg 2017).

Of course, to be able to "hear" the print, children have to first learn how to translate those little symbols on the page back into recognizable words. Even though the human brain does not naturally read and write, we *can* rewire our brains to recognize letters, and eventually familiar letter strings, automatically. But, to read and write, a fourth processing system must develop in our brains. The addition of the print processing system—the *orthographic processing system*—completes what is referred to as reading's Four-Part Processing Model. This system is illustrated in Figure 1.2.

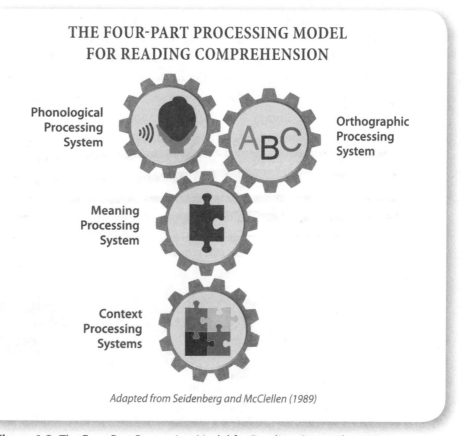

THE FOUR-PART PROCESSING MODEL
FOR READING COMPREHENSION

Phonological Processing System

Orthographic Processing System

Meaning Processing System

Context Processing Systems

Adapted from Seidenberg and McClellen (1989)

Figure 1.2 The Four-Part Processing Model for Reading Comprehension

We'll study this critical system throughout this book. For now, what's important to know is that the orthographic processing system adds print input to the already up-and-running language comprehension system so that our brains can "listen" to what we read, comprehend it, and acquire even more vocabulary, structure and knowledge. Sense-making in written text, then, depends on the reader recognizing enough of the language of the text to hear and understand what they are reading (Seidenberg 2017; Wolf 2007).

MISUNDERSTANDING:

If children have strong oral language, they have most of what they need to learn to read.

Clearly strong reading comprehension depends on strong listening comprehension. But there is certainly more to reading success than being able to understand spoken language. So, what does it take to learn to read?

The Simple View of Reading, commonly referred to as SVR, provides a framework for understanding the way word reading (decoding or automatic word recognition) and listening comprehension (also referred to as language comprehension) both factor into the ultimate goal, reading comprehension (Adlof, Catts, and Little 2006; Dreyer and Katz 1992; Gough and Tunmer 1986; Hoover and Gough 1990; Joshi and Aaron 2000). The Simple View is presented as a mathematical equation, as shown in Figure 1.3.

In this equation, reading comprehension is represented as the product of two separate but equally important skills. If either of these skills is limited or missing altogether, the whole system—reading comprehension, or *sense-making*—breaks down. For example, if a child does not have the listening comprehension necessary to understand a particular text—that is, the child would not understand

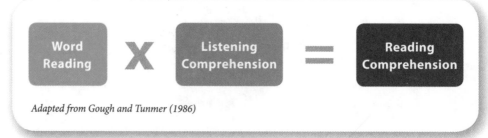

Adapted from Gough and Tunmer (1986)

FIGURE 1.3 Simple View of Reading Equation

that text if someone read it aloud—then reading comprehension for that text is out of reach. No amount of word recognition skill will compensate for the limitations a child's listening comprehension puts on reading comprehension (Cervetti et. al 2020).

On the other hand, even with sufficient listening comprehension, if a child doesn't have adequate skills for figuring out the print—decoding—the child will not be able to comprehend the spoken language the print represents. You can't comprehend what you can't read. It's that simple.

So, supporting students in becoming successful readers requires careful attention to both sides of the reading comprehension equation—decoding or recognizing the words (word reading) and understanding spoken language (listening comprehension). Scarborough's Rope is a metaphor that elaborates on these two essential components of reading, offering substrands that make the rope strong (Scarborough 2001). Table 1.2 lists these critical substrands.

TABLE 1.2

SUBSTRANDS OF SCARBOROUGH'S READING ROPE

Substrands of the Word Recognition Rope (Word Reading)	Substrands of the Language Comprehension Rope (Listening Comprehension)
Phonological awareness Decoding Sight recognition of familiar words	Background knowledge Vocabulary Language structures Verbal reasoning Literacy knowledge

Adapted from Scarborough (2001)

These two categories of skill, listening comprehension and word reading, although each important in its own right, must ultimately weave together. They form a rope that gets stronger and stronger as the chords of word recognition and sense-making become increasingly automatic. Inattention to any of the threads in Table 1.2 will potentially affect the end goal—reading comprehension.

MISUNDERSTANDING:

Successful comprehension in beginning reading texts means that reading comprehension is on track.

For beginning readers who need to get started reading with simple texts—"A pup can run and jump!"—it can often appear that they have strong reading comprehension. However, the simple language demands of these texts can temporarily mask reading comprehension difficulties.

> *In the early grades, the texts used to assess reading comprehension and follow-up comprehension questions demand less from one's language system, which allows those with weak language skills to read simple texts and answer basic comprehension questions as accurately as their typically developing peers. (Hogan, Adlof, and Alonzo 2014, 201–202)*

Beginning readers usually have listening comprehension skills that exceed the demands of these simple texts, so if they can decode the texts, chances are they can understand them.

Therefore, comprehension problems—which tend to be linked to limited language skills—often stay hidden until later grades (Nation et al. 2004) when the complexity of the texts begins to exceed the limits of a child's listening comprehension (Catts, Hogan, and Adlof 2005; Curtis 1980).

Let us explain.

As students become more adept at decoding, they move into increasingly complex texts. These texts contain words and ideas that require more sophisticated language. So, developing more competence with decoding can actually reveal a different barrier—language. In fact, by eighth grade, nearly all of the reading comprehension differences between readers can be attributed not to differences in decoding but to differences in listening comprehension (Adlof, Catts, and Little 2006).

Given the simplicity of beginning reading texts, is it any wonder that, around third grade, we notice more difficulties with reading comprehension, as text gets significantly more complex and comprehension demands increase?

As Figure 1.4 illustrates, as word recognition becomes more and more automatic through the grades, access to complex language and ideas increasingly shifts from listening comprehension to reading comprehension.

This diagram can help us understand why the oral language of young children so accurately predicts later reading comprehension (Castles, Rastle, and Nation 2018). This same correlation highlights the critical importance of language development opportunities, because they feed later comprehension of more and more complex texts.

In typically developing readers, listening comprehension and reading comprehension eventually become one and the same. So, children struggling with comprehension need *more* than comprehension strategies. They need abundant opportunities to use and develop language and to build knowledge. In fact, knowledge can even outweigh strategy use when it comes to reading comprehension, as was demonstrated in a classic study where children who struggled with reading but knew a lot about baseball outperformed their peers who were proficient readers but knew little about baseball (Recht and Leslie 1988)!

What does this mean for teachers in the primary grades? It means that in the early years, while children are learning to read—with texts that are necessarily well below their listening comprehension capacity—we must have an eye toward the future, focusing on stretching the limits of listening comprehension through oral language development and knowledge building.

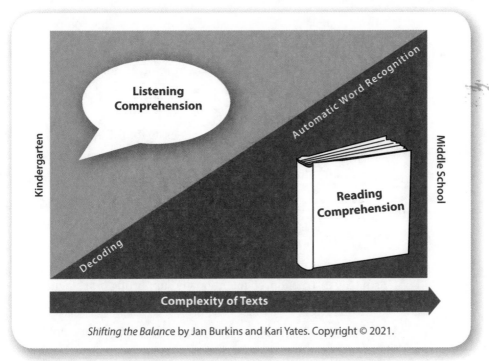

Shifting the Balance by Jan Burkins and Kari Yates. Copyright © 2021.

FIGURE 1.4 Access to Complex Language and Opportunities for Deep Thinking

This work can be done through regular and rich interactive read-aloud, through storytelling, through purposeful use of complex vocabulary, through opportunities for experiential learning, by intentional content area instruction, and by making space for meaningful conversation across the school day.

The work of helping children learn the phonetic code to bring their orthographic processing system online—completing the brain's mechanisms for the Four-Part Processing Model—is pressing work of the early grades. But it is urgently important that we continually nourish the other three language systems as well, ensuring that efficient word recognition is not developed only to later be brought to a grinding halt by language comprehension limitations down the road.

A Short Summary of the Science

- ▲ In the brain, listening comprehension develops through the work of three interconnected processing systems—phonological, meaning, and context.

- ▲ Print is spoken language written down. So listening comprehension is important for reading comprehension.

- ▲ The orthographic processing system, which comes online when children learn to read, receives input through print and completes the Four-Part Processing Model.

- ▲ Word recognition skills can't compensate for the limitations a child's listening comprehension puts on reading comprehension (Simple View of Reading).

- ▲ As word recognition becomes more and more automatic, access to complex language and ideas through reading comprehension increases.

- ▲ Strong oral language can reduce the need for comprehension strategy instruction, so intentionally supporting oral language development in the classroom is important.

- ▲ It is important that beginning readers have access to complex ideas through read-aloud, conversation, content area instruction, and other language-developing opportunities.

THE SIMPLE AND SCIENTIFICALLY SOUND SHIFT

Treat oral language development as an essential ingredient for comprehension.

Recommendations for Making the Shift

Given how important listening comprehension is for later reading comprehension, it is imperative that we intentionally support oral language development in the classroom.

In this section, we offer some suggestions for doing just that—maximizing early listening comprehension so that later reading comprehension interventions are necessary less often.

Gather what you need to support language comprehension.

1. **Read-aloud texts.** Choose texts that will stretch listening comprehension by providing exposure to rich ideas, wide vocabulary, background knowledge, and novel language structures.

2. **Text sets** built around a particular topic or theme, representing a range of text complexity. These text sets will provide multiple entry points for students to build background knowledge, acquire language structures, and expand vocabulary around key topics (Liben and Liben 2019).

3. A collection of **high-leverage instructional routines** for building and extending both intentional and incidental classroom conversations. We offer several key instructional routines in Table 1.3, and zoom in on three of them: reading aloud, using interesting words, and planned and incidental conversations.

Learn to use a few high-leverage instructional routines to build language.

Routines for building speaking and listening skills are easily woven across the entire learning day. These instructional strategies do not require fancy materials, specialized training, or big schedule changes. They simply require a commitment to be intentional about bringing the classroom alive with spoken language and conversation. In Table 1.3, we offer some suggestions for you to explore. After the table, we zoom in on the use of interesting words, interactive read alouds, and repeating and expanding on what children say.

TABLE 1.3

HIGH-LEVEL INSTRUCTIONAL ROUTINES FOR LANGUAGE DEVELOPMENT

The What: *Routine*	The Why: *Purpose*	The How: *Examples*
Make space for planned and incidental conversation.	To leverage conversation throughout the day (transitions, turn-and-talk, morning greetings, etc.) and give children practice articulating ideas, listening, adding on, and asking relevant questions	"Let's talk about …" "This is so interesting. Let's talk more about it …" "Tell us about what just happened." "Talk to your partner about …" "Who wants to add on to _____?"
Ask quality questions.	To ensure that students have opportunities for higher-level thinking, such as describing, explaining, comparing, evaluating, and inferring	"What do you think about …?" "How are _____ and _____ alike or different?" "Why do you think that is more important?" "Explain what really happened."
Provide wait time.	To give children the time they need to process information, formulate thoughts, and organize their language to express their ideas	After posing a question, wait. (Silence.) "I'll give you some time to think about what you want to say." "Let your partner think."
Repeat and expand.	To reinforce, extend, and clarify student language	"Wow, that's so interesting. You had …" "So you …" "I don't understand. Tell me more about …"

continues

The What: *Routine*	The Why: *Purpose*	The How: *Examples*
Use interesting words.	To teach new vocabulary and encourage students to use it, and to teach children to notice and acquire new words	"Let's all be on the lookout for new and interesting words." "Let's take some time to learn this powerful word." "Let's see if we can all find ways to use this word today."
Read aloud.	To introduce students to new vocabulary, to build background knowledge, to expose children to language and text structures, and to provide children joyful experiences with books	"Let's read this book to see what we can learn about _____." "Let's read this sentence again and try to figure out what it means." "Why did you love this story?" "What's worth talking more about?" "Tell the story to your partner in your own words."
Teach with text sets to build content area knowledge.	To use text sets across read-aloud and shared, guided, and independent reading—including that in content area instruction—to build background knowledge about and interest in a topic	"Today we're going to learn more about _____ by reading _____." "Let's start a basket for all the books we are collecting about _____." "You'll be excited to find some of the same words and ideas from the other book(s) we've read. Tell us about the connections you find."

Zooming In on the Use of Interesting Words

Every time you talk to students, you make choices about which words to share with them. Don't hesitate or shy away from using big, bold, audacious words. You don't have to water language down for children. Using strong vocabulary will not only make your kids feel respected, but once you've planted the seeds in students' phonological lexicons—where the brain collects every word it has ever heard—you've increased the chance that they will develop an understanding of it, try it out for themselves, and even recognize it when they encounter it in print.

Exposing students to new words can include the language of practical life in the classroom—such as asking children to *gather* or *assemble* on the carpet rather than to simply *go to the carpet*. It can also include academic language—*quotation marks* versus *talking marks*, *observe* versus *watch*, *synchronous* versus *at the same time*—and vocabulary that is specific to content-area subjects—*cocoon*, *government*, *metamorphosis*. Remember, exposure to interesting words now is an investment in future reading comprehension.

To help children come to know words more completely, consider ways of knowing that support all four of the processing systems:

- ▲ **Phonological** Have children listen carefully to each of the sounds in the pronunciation of the word, and then say the word several times themselves, hearing each sound—feeling them in their mouths—and the full pronunciation of the word.

- ▲ **Meaning** Share a simple definition of the word, including a visual or a metaphor if helpful. Have students say the word again and tell a friend what it means in their own words.

- ▲ **Context** Use the word in the context of a sentence. Have children do the same. Offer multiple examples of how the word is used.

- ▲ **Orthographic** Look at the features of the written word, even if many of them represent phonics concepts not yet familiar to the age group. Say the word slowly again, as you match the sounds to the spellings.

Whether words are discovered during read-aloud or independent reading, during a science lesson, or through conversation, children will be excited to keep a record of the new and interesting words they are learning. You can use a chart, a collection of index cards, or student word logs. Even if they can't read them all, seeing, hearing, and understanding the meaning of these words sets up children's language processing systems for listening and reading comprehension success.

Zooming In on Interactive Read-Aloud

When it comes to language development, read-aloud is one of your most powerful tools (Layne 2015, McCarthy 2020). Interactive read-aloud provides an important bridge between spoken and written language, combining a more conversational guided experience with the more complex and formal language of books. And it's not news to you that picture books are a robust source of interesting words, complex language structures, and engaging information. In fact, when compared with the language adults typically use with children, new or unusual words and language structures are more prevalent in most books for children (Montag, Jones, and Smith 2015). Of course, "most books" does not mean *all* books. The more intentional we are about the books we read aloud and how we engage children in talking about them, the more they will benefit children's language development (Swanson et al. 2011). So, to get even more language learning bang for your buck, we offer the following read-aloud tips:

▲ **Choose texts with more complex ideas, words, and language structures** than most of your children would be able to read for themselves (Burkins and Yaris 2016; Yates 2015). This may sometimes involve connecting to science or social studies content.

▲ **Preview texts for interesting and unfamiliar vocabulary worth exploring with children.** Consider both:

▶ Which new words are critical to the understanding of *this* text?
▶ Which new words are possible high-leverage words for use in the future?

▲ **Get comfortable using a parenthetical explanation of high-utility vocabulary** on the run. This gives students a bit of information about an important word, without a complete break from the flow of the story. For example, "Trudy looked out at the horizon (that means the place where the earth meets the sky) stretching her eyes for any sign of papa and his wagon."

▲ **Plan for meaningful conversation points in the texts,** using high-quality questions and thoughtful use of wait time (Burkins and Yaris 2016; Yates 2015). Rich texts are full of rich ideas and information, and processing through conversation will deepen students' understanding of the text.

▲ **Have students utilize high-quality turn-and-talk practices** (Yates 2015) that include turn taking, active listening, checking for understanding, and prompting each other for elaboration. (Yes, even kindergarteners can learn to do this—and what better life skill could we focus on than helping kids become strong conversational partners?)

Zooming In on Repeating and Expanding

Some of the most compelling research on building young children's oral language is that of Grover Whitehurst and colleagues (1988), who have repeatedly demonstrated (and others have confirmed) that a few simple practices can increase the oral language of children by many months (Hargrave and Sénéchal 2000; Lever and Sénéchal 2011).

We can carry these practices into K–2 classrooms by repeating and expanding what students say in response to questions we ask during a read-aloud or conversations. We've adapted Whitehurst and colleagues' strategy to develop a dialogic conversations tool. The steps in dialogic conversations are simple to understand but require practice to implement fluently. Figure 1.5 includes descriptions of the steps in the process, a sample conversation, and some tips for trying out this process yourself.

Once you get the hang of dialogic conversation during read-aloud, you will find you can use it across the day in both academic and personal conversations with students. Whatever their language proficiency, you can meet students wherever they are and elevate their language. To download a PDF of this tool, go to **TheSixShifts.com**/downloadables.

DIALOGIC CONVERSATIONS: PROCESS, SAMPLE, AND TIPS

1. Engage

Engage children in a verbal interaction around a text or just in general conversation. This may involve asking the child's opinion, asking the child to name or recall something from a text, asking the child to make connections to personal experience.

2. Repeat

Repeat what children say, embedding this in your response in a natural way. If the student's response includes a mistake, only repeat the correct part or integrate a correction into this step.

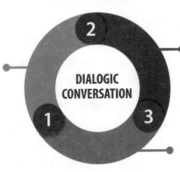

3. Expand

As you repeat, say a little more than what the child said. Expand the language to include a new word, phrase, or idea. Then begin the process again!

Sample Prompts:

- What are you thinking about?
- How did you celebrate?
- What was your favorite part?
- What did you do last night?
- What do you think .... means?

SAMPLE DIALOGIC READING CONVERSATION

1 Engage — What was your favorite part of the book?

When the mouse saved the lion.

2 Repeat **&** **3** Expand — Oh, when the mouse saved the lion! That was surprising!

1 Engage — How do you think the mouse felt?

Happy!

DIALOGIC CONVERSATION TIPS

1. Adjust your responses and language based on the age of the child.
2. Make your conversation authentic. Show interest in the child, the conversation, and/or the text.
3. Be intentional! This process is simple to understand but takes intentionality and practice.

Adapted from Whitehurst et al. (1988).

FIGURE 1.5 Dialogic Conversations: Process, Sample, and Tips

▲ ▼ ▼ ▼ ▼ ▼

Meanwhile, Back in the Classroom . . .

Lakeside Elementary has recently begun to focus on classroom strategies that will support language development, not just for the many English learners that attend the school, but for all students. This focus is driven in part by an ongoing concern about third- and fourth-grade reading comprehension scores. Beginning in January, every teacher in the school is committing to one new strategy from a menu of options to support language development in the classroom.

Because Mr. Tucker already places a high value on personally greeting every student at the door in the morning, he sees an opportunity to enhance this routine by being purposeful about having dialogic conversations with a couple of students each morning. With each one, he engages, listens, repeats, expands, and then volleys the conversation back to the student.

Although he was concerned at first that the strategy might feel forced or unnatural, it was clear from the start that this strategy was good not only for language development but also for deepening relationships with students. He's finding that his intentional efforts in the morning have made him more aware of the ways he engages children with language throughout the day. Six weeks in, Mr. Tucker finds this language expansion strategy so powerful that he's decided to make it a regular part of his read-aloud and has even experimented with it during science. He's been surprised by how much of the science of weather his students have recently learned.

In the lunchroom, as he shares his success with a colleague, she chimes in that, although she'd chosen a different focus, she, too, was truly excited. "I haven't done anything fancy. I just got really intentional about bringing more interesting vocabulary into the lives of my kids every day in two ways—through my own conversations with them and by strategically choosing read-alouds with really rich vocabulary. I said to the kids, 'Let's all try to learn and use more interesting words every day.' I've been pleasantly surprised at how excited my children have become about learning new and interesting words."

Questions for Reflection

Checking In with Yourself: Which of the misunderstandings in this shift did you find yourself thinking most deeply about? What might be the next step for you?

Classroom Conversation: How can you expand students' opportunities to engage in meaningful classroom conversations?

Read Aloud: How often do you read aloud to students? Do the texts you select include rich vocabulary and language structures? How do you make space for student conversation and contributions during the read-aloud?

Building Knowledge: How can you use themed or connected texts in strategic ways to intentionally build students' background knowledge? Is there science or social studies content that you can support during read-aloud? How will you leverage your content area instruction to build students' background knowledge?

Engaging, Repeating, Expanding: How will you adopt and practice these three dialogic conversation moves to the point of fluency? What critical friend can you engage to support your practice and give you feedback?

Modeling: How can you integrate more extensive vocabulary into the language of the classroom? How can you model a love for words and teach children to notice, collect, and use new and interesting words?

Differentiation: Who do your current practices best serve? Who will benefit the most from a shift in practice?

Recommitting to Phonemic Awareness Instruction

Ms. Martin has mixed emotions at the weekly meeting of her professional learning community. Her literacy coach is helping the kindergarten team walk through their winter assessment results. On one hand, there's much to celebrate about the progress students have made with learning letter names and sounds. The formative classroom data Ms. Martin collected from her students seem to align with the district's formal screening data. It feels good to get confirmation that her consistent and differentiated approach to teaching letter names and sounds has paid off. Tia, for example, really stands out, having gone from knowing only two letter names (*T* and *X*) and no sounds, to knowing twenty-three letters and sixteen sounds.

Ms. Martin is also excited to reflect on the progress her students have made on the district-designed, informal concepts about print measure. She attributes the growth on this measure to her daily commitment to shared reading with a variety of big books, poems, and charts.

But when it comes to the district's phoneme segmentation assessment, Ms. Martin quickly sees that she has many children who are below, or well below, expected benchmark targets. Although she is not surprised by every name in the "at-risk" categories, she is quite puzzled by some, especially those who already know most of their letter names and sounds. Again, Tia stands out. Her progress with letter names and sounds doesn't seem to align with her worrisome phoneme segmentation score at all. And Jonah—who came to school knowing nearly all of his letters and sounds—has the lowest score in the class on this measure.

Ms. Martin wonders: *Was this really a valid measure of what my kids can do? Could it have been a bad testing day for some of them? What is the real importance of phoneme segmentation, anyway? And what about my kids who could already do some beginning decoding; did they really still need to focus on this seemingly minute skill, phoneme segmentation?*

As they reflect together, Ms. Martin finds that many of her colleagues have similar wonderings and doubts about the phoneme segmentation assessment. But when they do a round-robin reflection about their intentional efforts with phonemic awareness instruction, Ms. Martin notices something else.

Together, the teachers' responses start to sound a bit like a recipe for stone soup, adding a bit of this and a bit of that—a few poems, some rhyming games, some syllable clapping, a sound-sorting activity—mix them together and hope for the best.

As she listens to the conversation, she also notices some of her teammates use the term *phonological awareness,* and others use *phonemic awareness.* One even seems to use *phonemic awareness* and *phonics* interchangeably. She realizes she's a bit foggy on the differences between these terms herself.

Her colleague, Mrs. Winston, who recently joined the team from another district, laments the lack of a structured phonemic awareness curriculum and explains that in her previous district, they had a dedicated twenty-minute block of whole-group phonemic awareness instruction daily. Ms. Martin thinks about the diverse needs of her own students and has serious concerns about whether adding a big block of whole-group instruction will be the right answer for them.

The one thing everyone seems to agree on—time and money are in short supply. Whatever next steps they choose will have to be low investment and high return.

As Ms. Martin walks to the gym to pick up her students, she finds herself getting more curious about what those phoneme segmentation results really mean and how she might be able to use them to adjust her instruction.

2

A COMMON PRACTICE
TO RECONSIDER

▼ ▲ ▼ ▼ ▼ ▼

*Taking a "bit-of-this-and-a-bit-of-that" approach
to phonemic awareness instruction.*

Ms. Martin is not alone in wondering about the role of phonemic awareness. It's on the minds of many teachers of beginning readers these
days, ourselves included. And, as we've taken a fresh look at the body of science around this topic (some that's new, and some that's been around for several decades now), we've had to ask ourselves: Could it be that we are missing
(or misunderstanding) some compelling opportunities to build a bridge
between phonemic awareness research and instructional practice in early literacy classrooms? It seems that the answer is yes.

Clearing Up Some Confusion

One of the most critical opportunities to begin rethinking, rebuilding, and
rebalancing our beginning reading practice may be in providing more robust
and intentional phonemic awareness instruction. Volumes of compelling
research point to the fact that phonemic awareness instruction—teaching children to notice, articulate, and manipulate the smallest sounds in words—can
pay huge dividends in getting readers off to a stronger start with both reading
and writing (Brady 2020; Clayton et al. 2020; Suggate 2016).

So, let's take a look at some common misunderstandings about phonemic
awareness and the reasons we may want to rethink them.

2

MISUNDERSTANDING:

Phonemic awareness develops naturally.

As we learned in Chapter 1, oral language provides humans a powerful tool-box for communication, allowing us to choose words from an array of possibilities. Our precise language choices allow us to communicate our ideas with detail, nuance, spice, and emotion. Our words enrich our lives, shape our stories, and strengthen our connections with others.

But prior to *written* language, our ancestors needed to be face-to-face to use language. This was a definite limitation, driving a relentless search for ways to share language across time and space. And although primitive drawings and pictographs were a step in the right direction, they definitely did not lend themselves to capturing complex ideas or precise wording. Thank goodness for the persistence of scholars across the globe, whose trial, error, and tenacity eventually resulted in the invention of a written alphabet (Sacks 2003; Wolf 2007).

So, what does the invention of written language have to do with phonemic awareness, anyway? Well, pretty much everything.

You see, the invention of our modern-day alphabet was made possible by our ancestors' discovery of phonemes. Scholars figured out that they could freeze spoken language in print by

1. breaking every word apart into its tiniest little sound bits, and

2. representing each of those separate sounds with an abstract symbol.

Ultimately, people could learn all of these little symbols and the sounds that went with each one. Then they'd be able to use the special code to freeze-dry (write) precise ideas that could later be reconstituted (read) back into speech, which the language processing systems could then hear and make sense of. Because *you* read and write the same special code that *we* do—the Latin alphabet— you are able to unlock the ideas we have left for you on this page.

On this side of history, it may seem obvious, but the discovery of this idea— that words are made up of little sounds that can be individually represented with symbols—was a monumental, intellectual feat. It at last provided the path for human beings to say absolutely anything in one time and space and then unlock it word for word in a completely different time and space (Adams 1990; Dehaene 2009; Sacks 2003; Wolf 2007; Moats and Tolman 2019). Figure 2.1 represents this powerful process, which most of us have come to take for granted.

FROM SPEECH TO PRINT TO SPEECH

Shifting the Balance by Jan Burkins and Kari Yates. Copyright © 2021.

FIGURE 2.1 From Speech to Print to Speech

Of course, there is at least one catch with any system of written language: *People have to learn to use the system*! And although human brains have always been able to learn spoken language with relative ease, they are *not* naturally wired for many of the demands that the invention of *written* language placed upon them (Wolf 2007; Seidenberg 2017).

Slowing speech down to notice and manipulate the tiny sounds embedded in words is anything but natural. One reason for this is that spoken language is more or less continuous (Adams 1990; Morais et al. 1986, 1979).

In much the same way that it is difficult to distinguish where one color in a rainbow ends and another begins, sounds, and even words, blend, bump into, and bleed all over each other in ways that are not at all simple to untangle. This is called *coarticulation.* In other words, phonemes, syllables, words, and even phrases have a whole lot of boundary issues, which can make developing phonemic awareness tricky for children.

To develop awareness of phonemes, we have to rewire our brains, retraining our phonological processing systems for a new job. This new job involves learning to listen inside of words for tiny, little, mostly meaningless bits called *phonemes.* It includes pulling the sounds in spoken language apart, fishing them out individually, swapping or rearranging them, and putting them back together. There is no practical reason for your brain to do all this abstract work . . . unless you want to learn to read and write in an alphabetic system.

As students step into literacy, the act of learning to efficiently untangle, discriminate, segment, blend, and manipulate those tiny little sound slices called phonemes becomes paramount (Liberman et al. 1967; Liberman et al. 1974; Melby-Lervåg, Lyster, and Hulme 2012). The phonological processing system's new line of work represents a drastic shift from its prior experiences with oral language, which have been *all* and *only* about meaning making. This is because most phonemes are meaningless in their own right.

Basically, phonemic awareness involves coming to understand that the word *duck* has three sounds, none of which is *quack* (Adams 1990; Wolf 2007). But as hard as this new job is for our brains, research clearly shows, with instruction, our brains can learn to listen for the sounds within words (Adams 1990; Bus and van IJzendoorn 1999; Ehri et al. 2001; Kilpatrick 2015; Melby-Lervåg, Lyster, and Hulme 2012; Miller 1999; Snow, Burns, and Griffin 1998).

MISUNDERSTANDING:

Phonemic awareness and phonics are the same thing.

It is easy to confuse phonics and phonemic awareness, not just because they both start with *phon* (which means sound) but also because their roles have a great deal of overlap. Phonemic awareness and phonics are reciprocal skill sets that can *and* should be woven together in complementary ways. So work on phonemic awareness tends to help children with learning phonics, and, on the flip side, work learning letters and sounds tends to develop phonemic awareness (Brady 2020); Castles and Coltheart 2004; Clayton et al. 2020; Hulme et al. 2012). Nevertheless, phonemic awareness and phonics are each important aspects of learning to read in their own right, and each demands its own intentional instruction (Brady 2020; Kjeldsen,et al. 2014).

The most basic distinction between phonics and phonemic awareness is the inclusion (or exclusion) of letters (Adams 1990). Phonemic awareness, in its purest sense, involves only spoken sounds, without letters attached. Once you add letters to the sounds, the phonemic awareness work begins to overlap with phonics work. So identifying the first *sound* in the word *cat* as /k/ is phonemic awareness work. On the other hand, identifying the first *letter* in *cat* as *C* is phonics work (although it requires the phonemic awareness work of isolating the initial phoneme).

To complicate matters further, there is a third *phon-* term in this tricky mix: *phonological awareness*. Phonemic awareness is actually a subset of phonological awareness. More specifically, phonemic awareness is phonological awareness work *at the phoneme level,* or with the smallest unit of speech, the phoneme. We offer Table 2.1 to serve as a reference for keeping these three *phon-* words straight in your mind and in your conversations.

TABLE 2.1

PHON- INSTRUCTION FOR BEGINNING READERS: *KEEPING IT STRAIGHT*

phon- Word	What Is It?	Examples of Instruction
Phonological awareness instruction	Phonological awareness is the umbrella term for any work helping students learn to notice and/or manipulate sounds in speech. This includes work on the word, syllable, and phoneme levels (phonemic awareness). However, it is commonly used to refer more narrowly to work that is not on the phoneme level.	• Identifying how many words are in a sentence • Clapping the syllables in a word • Identifying and producing rhyming words • Segmenting or blending the two components of compound words
Phonemic awareness instruction	Phonemic awareness is a subcategory of phonological awareness. It is the more specific work of helping students learn to articulate, notice, and manipulate the *individual* speech sounds (phonemes) in words.	• Using a mirror to notice what the mouth, lips, and tongue are doing when producing different phonemes • Blending separate phonemes together into one cohesive word • Breaking a word apart into individual phonemes • Deleting one phoneme from a word and replacing it with a different phoneme
Phonics instruction	Phonics is helping students learn the relationships between the sounds (phonemes) in our spoken language and the symbols (graphemes) that represent them.	• Identifying letter names • Identifying letter sounds • Using decoding to unlock written words • Using encoding to translate spoken words into written words

MISUNDERSTANDING:

Once children know all their letters and sounds, they will be able to read.

As we design instruction for young students, it seems obvious *and* intuitive that if children are going to learn to unlock the code of written language, they are going to need to learn all of the pairings between those special symbols and the phonemes that they represent. But, teaching letter names and sounds (phonics) without a strong and intentional focus on helping kids learn to pry spoken words apart and put them back together (phonemic awareness) might be one of the places that our early literacy instruction is a bit out of balance.

Early print instruction, or phonics, is an important component of learning to read. But phonemic awareness is equally important, if not more important, in the very earliest stages of reading development (Elbro 1996; Blachman 1995, 2000; Torgesen 2002). In fact, all children who learn to read successfully have phonemic awareness, and most children with dyslexia have trouble with phonemic awareness (Blachman 1991; Brady 1986; Bus and IJzendoorn 1999; Cooney and Swanson 1987; Ehri et al. 2001; Kilpatrick 2015; Lundberg, Frost, and Peterson 1988; National Early Literacy Panel 2008; National Institute of Child Health and Human Development 2000; Snow, Burns, and Griffin 1998; Wagner and Torgeson 1987). So, to enter the world of reading and writing, each and every child must make the same discovery our ancestors made. That is, every child must have their *own* "light bulb moment" when suddenly they understand the following critical truths about our alphabetic system of written language.

- ▲ Every spoken word can be broken apart into phonemes—the tiniest bits of speech.

- ▲ Every written word is made up of specific symbols from our alphabet.

- ▲ Every sound in a spoken word is represented by a letter (or combination of letters) in a written word, and vice versa.

This collective understanding, referred to by researchers as the *alphabetic principle* (Byrne and Fielding-Barnsley 1989; Byrne 2005), is illustrated in Figure 2.2.

From our vantage point as proficient readers, these understandings may seem incredibly obvious, but for children who are not yet readers, they are anything but. Yet the moment when children reach the critical "aha" of clearly

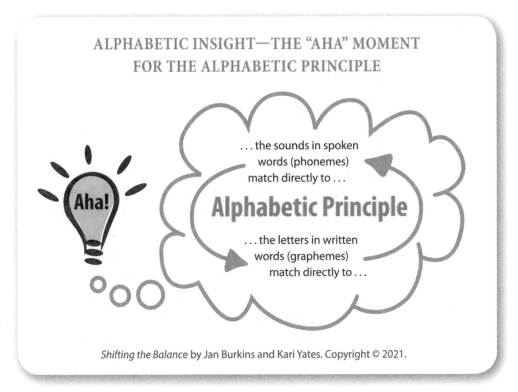

ALPHABETIC INSIGHT—THE "AHA" MOMENT
FOR THE ALPHABETIC PRINCIPLE

Aha!

. . . the sounds in spoken
words (phonemes)
match directly to . . .

Alphabetic Principle

. . . the letters in written
words (graphemes)
match directly to . . .

Shifting the Balance by Jan Burkins and Kari Yates. Copyright © 2021.

FIGURE 2.2 Alphabetic Insight—The "Aha" Moment for the Alphabetic Principle

understanding the relationships among spoken words, sounds, and symbols— *alphabetic insight*—is the moment they are ready to take off with reading and writing.

Prior to alphabetic insight (Castles, Rastle, and Nation 2018), children like Tia and Jonah, from the beginning of this chapter, despite knowing the names and sounds of many letters, are still likely to struggle to apply this knowledge as they attempt to read and write. But as Tia and Jonah also develop a firm understanding of the architectural sound structure of words through phonemic awareness instruction and practice, they will be positioned for their own "aha" moment about the ways speech and print are connected.

So, learning the letters and sounds alone is clearly insufficient for success in learning to read! Helping students discover (alphabetic insight) and deepen their understanding of the alphabetic principle, therefore, requires thoughtful emphasis on phonics *and* phonemic awareness—and their relationship—as two parallel and reciprocal sides of the beginning reading coin (Castles et al. 2009; Hulme et al. 2012; Miller 1999).

MISUNDERSTANDING:

Phonemic awareness is mostly a readiness or prereading skill.

The idea that children will benefit from some degree of instruction in phonemic awareness seems to be something most of us can agree on. However, in many cases it seems phonemic awareness is viewed as a readiness skill that students outgrow. Yet the truth is that phonemic awareness plays a vital role for all readers throughout their lifetimes, and students are still developing their phonemic awareness skills into the upper elementary grades (Kilpatrick 2015).

Phonemic awareness helps children develop automaticity with blending phonemes into words, segmenting words into phonemes to write them (encoding), and even moving sight words into long-term memory. Without phonemic awareness, readers can't develop reading fluency or "hear" words in their minds to comprehend text (Ehri 2005a, 2005b, 2014; Gentry and Ouellette 2019; Gough and Tunmer 1986; Kilpatrick 2015; Lervåg and Aukrust 2010; National Institute of Child Health and Human Development 2000; Oakhill, Cain, and Bryant 2003; Perfetti, Landi, and Oakhill 2005).

Since phonemic awareness is a thread that winds through many interwoven aspects of learning to read and write, it is no surprise that children who have difficulty developing an awareness of phonemes are much more likely to have reading and writing difficulties. In fact, research confirms that a lack of strong phonemic awareness is a contributing factor to the majority of reading difficulties (Blachman 1995, 2000; Torgesen 2002). But the reverse is also true: with early and intentional instruction in phonemic awareness, many reading difficulties can be avoided altogether (Kilpatrick 2015; National Institute of Child Health and Human Development 2000; Torgesen 2002).

MISUNDERSTANDING:

Intentional phonemic awareness instruction takes a lot of time or fancy resources.

While we strategize and search for solutions that will meet the needs of young children, it's easy to think to ourselves, "If only we had more time and more money, just imagine what we could do!" Yet the reality of life in schools is that time and money will probably always be in short supply. Luckily, phonemic awareness instruction requires a surprisingly low investment for an immense return. So, what is the investment?

You can get started teaching phonemic awareness with just a few minutes a day and a clear understanding of the most important tasks (Table 2.2), including an awareness of what makes each of them easier or harder for children (Table 2.3). Research has demonstrated that consistency is more important than quantity. A teacher's knowledge of these relationships between phonemic awareness skills, used to thoughtfully design instruction, can actually reduce the amount of time it takes for students to develop phonemic awareness by up to 40 percent (Kjeldsen et al. 2014). So, individual phonemic awareness lessons must be held together by a larger, intentional plan of instruction which doesn't have to come from a program, although it can (Melby-Lervåg, Lyster, and Hulme 2012). Table 2.2 describes the important phonemic awareness tasks in order of difficulty and offers some sample language for each.

TABLE 2.2

EXAMPLES OF PHONEMIC AWARENESS TASKS FROM LESS TO MORE DIFFICULT

	Definition	Example
Phoneme blending	Phoneme blending is taking separate sounds (phonemes) and putting them together seamlessly to make a single word.	Teacher: Listen while I say some sounds— /m/-/ ă /-/p/. Now you put them together to make the whole word. Student: map
Phoneme segmentation	Phoneme segmentation is breaking a word it into its individual sounds (phonemes).	Teacher: Listen while I say the word, *can*. Now you say each sound in the word, *can*. Student: /k/-/ă/-/n/
Phoneme isolation	Phoneme isolation is locating and separating one individual phoneme from the rest of the word.	Teacher: Say *clap*. Now say just the first (last, middle, second) sound in *clap*. Student: /k/

continues

	Definition	Example
Phoneme discrimination	Phoneme discrimination is hearing the similarities and/or differences in two or more phonemes, usually within words.	Teacher: Which word doesn't have the same beginning (ending, middle) sound as the others? *dog, door, put* Student: put
Phoneme deletion	Phoneme deletion is removing one phoneme from a word completely. Deletion can result in a new word or can be a preparatory step for substitution.	Teacher: Say *ram*. Student: ram Teacher: Now, say *ram* without the /r/. Student: am
Phoneme substitution	Phoneme substitution is removing one phoneme from a word and replacing it with another phoneme. Substitution is the most complex work because it combines segmentation, isolation, deletion, and finally blending.	Teacher: Say *log*. Student: log Teacher: Now change /g/ to /t/. Student: lot

Within each of these subcategories of phonemic awareness instruction, the practice words we use make the specific tasks easier or harder. For example, segmenting the word *fish* into its three phonemes is much easier than segmenting *brisk* into its five phonemes. Both the length of the word *brisk* and the fact that it contains blends at the beginning and end of the word increase the difficulty of hearing its internal sound structure (Brady 2020). Figure 2.3 illustrates the hierarchy of difficulty associated with the location of phonemes in words, beginning with the easiest phoneme placement to hear (numbered 1) and ending with the most difficult placement (numbered 4).

Phoneme placement in words is not the only variable that makes working with them easier or harder. Table 2.3 describes some other characteristics of phonemic awareness tasks that can make them more (or less) difficult for children.

FIGURE 2.3 The Relationship Between Phoneme Placement and Task Difficulty

TABLE 2.3

EASE AND DIFFICULTY OF PHONOLOGICAL AWARENESS TASKS

Characteristic	What Makes It Easier or Harder?
Size of language unit	Larger language units are easier to work with than smaller units (words vs. syllables).
Type of manipulation task	Blending tasks are generally easier than segmenting tasks (/k/-/ă/-/t/ = cat). Substitution tasks are the most complex because they involve segmenting, deleting, adding, and blending. (Change the /t/ in stop to /l/. What word does it make?)
Placement of phoneme in a word	Phonemes at the beginning of a word are the easiest to hear, with other phoneme positions increasing in difficulty in the general order of the list below: • Beginning (/p/ in pin) • Final (/g/ in bag) • Medial (vowel)(/ŭ/ in bug) • Internal consonants in blends or consonant clusters (/t/ in stripe or /n/ in wind.)

continues

Characteristic	What Makes It Easier or Harder?
How the phoneme is formed	Phonemes formed with the same place or manner of articulation (/p/ and /b/, /s/ and /z/, etc.) are more difficult to distinguish from each other than those that are articulated in distinctly different ways (/p/ and /m/, /d/ and /n/, etc.).
	Phonemes are formed with the lips, teeth, tongue, vocal cords, and air stream (articulatory gestures).
	Some phonemes are just harder to form (/r/ vs. /ŏ/) and/or discriminate (/f/ vs. /v/) than others.

By beginning with simpler tasks and building to increasingly more difficult tasks, we can reach the ultimate goal of students noticing—and then learning to manipulate—phonemes (Kilpatrick 2015). But to get them there, instruction may need to start with much larger segments of speech (phonological awareness)—sentences, words, and syllables—but move quickly to the smallest units, phonemes (phonemic awareness). Ideally, children will participate in a lot of phonological awareness practice in preschool, and you can jump into phonemic awareness lessons at the beginning of kindergarten.

The structure in Figure 2.4 can guide you as you gather formative assessment data from your students and make instructional decisions about the specific kinds of practice children might need. Keep these ideas in mind as you study the figure:

▲ Phonemic awareness development is not completely linear.

▲ Children can learn more than one skill at a time.

▲ The time line of student growth along the progression will vary from child to child.

▲ Work on the phoneme level should not to be delayed until students have full mastery of phonological awareness tasks with larger units of speech, such as rhyming and syllable clapping.

▲ Beginning in kindergarten and continuing through first grade (and even beyond), it is urgent for all students to have consistent opportunities to develop, deepen, and apply phoneme-level skills, such as phoneme segmentation or substitution.

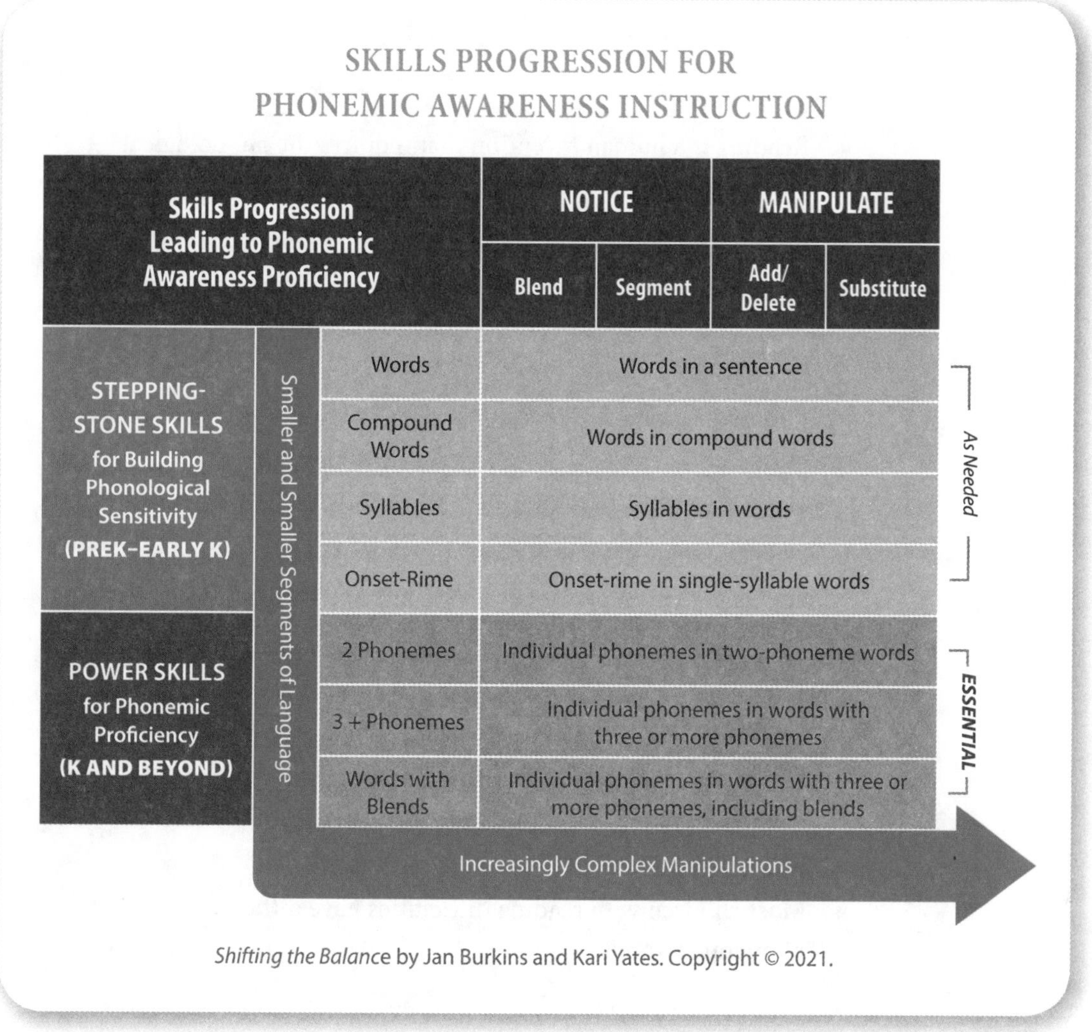

SKILLS PROGRESSION FOR PHONEMIC AWARENESS INSTRUCTION

Skills Progression Leading to Phonemic Awareness Proficiency			NOTICE		MANIPULATE	
			Blend	Segment	Add/ Delete	Substitute
STEPPING-STONE SKILLS for Building Phonological Sensitivity (PREK–EARLY K)	Smaller and Smaller Segments of Language	Words	Words in a sentence			
		Compound Words	Words in compound words			
		Syllables	Syllables in words			
		Onset-Rime	Onset-rime in single-syllable words			
POWER SKILLS for Phonemic Proficiency (K AND BEYOND)		2 Phonemes	Individual phonemes in two-phoneme words			
		3 + Phonemes	Individual phonemes in words with three or more phonemes			
		Words with Blends	Individual phonemes in words with three or more phonemes, including blends			

As Needed · *ESSENTIAL*

Increasingly Complex Manipulations

Shifting the Balance by Jan Burkins and Kari Yates. Copyright © 2021.

FIGURE 2.4 Skills Progression for Phonemic Awareness Instruction

So, you don't need to spend a lot of money purchasing fancy materials to teach phonemic awareness. Once you are equipped with these understandings of the hierarchy of phonemic awareness task, paired with the upcoming instructional recommendations, you will have what you need to get started with phonemic awareness instruction.

2

A Short Summary of the Science

- ▲ Reading is a human invention that requires the phonological processing system to learn a new job.

- ▲ Phonemic awareness can and should be taught.

- ▲ Phonemic awareness and phonics are *not* the same. Phonemic awareness and phonics involve reciprocal and complementary processes.

- ▲ Phonemic awareness is a subcategory of phonological awareness.

- ▲ Phonemic awareness should be the instructional priority, over phonological awareness tasks.

- ▲ Development of the alphabetic principle requires thoughtful attention to both phonemic awareness and early phonics.

- ▲ You can adjust the difficulty of phonemic awareness work by changing the task (blending vs. substitution), the word (*me* vs. *ramp*), or the position of the target phoneme (first, last, etc.).

- ▲ Evidence-based routines don't require large investments of money or time, but they do require an understanding of the hierarchy that makes tasks easier/harder.

- ▲ Most children with reading difficulties have difficulty with phonemic awareness.

THE SIMPLE AND SCIENTIFICALLY SOUND SHIFT

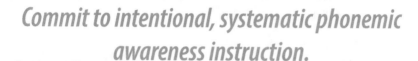

Commit to intentional, systematic phonemic awareness instruction.

Recommendations for Making the Shift

Given the many misunderstandings about phonemic awareness, you are probably wondering what you can do to make your instruction more focused and more intentional.

In this section, we offer a few suggestions you can use to help students both *notice* and *manipulate* the phonemic structure of individual words, using scientifically sound principles to guide you.

2

Gather what you need for thoughtful phonemic awareness instruction.

To teach phonemic awareness, you really need just a few things:

1. **Instructional Routines**

   A collection of **high-leverage instructional routines** for blending, segmenting, and phoneme manipulation. We offer a few instructional strategies in Table 2.4.

2. **Word Lists**

   A bank of words that lend themselves to each of the skill tasks. (Visit **TheSixShifts.com** for word lists.)

3. **Multisensory Scaffolds**

   Because phonemic awareness is abstract metalinguistic work, you will want to ensure that you make it more accessible by using multisensory and interactive scaffolds, such as moving chips or counters into Elkonin boxes or manipulating letter tiles or magnets (Elkonin 1973). Making the work multisensory is especially important when tasks are new or students are struggling.

4. **Assessment Plan**

   You need a thoughtful assessment plan and tools to monitor student progress and inform your reteaching and differentiation efforts.

Learn to use a few high-leverage instructional routines.

Because you can do them on the run with few or no materials, phonemic awareness tasks are easy to weave across the school day and can even be playful and engaging. Table 2.4 highlights fun and practical opportunities for teaching phonemic awareness as well as some sample instructional language. In the sections after the table, we zoom in on articulatory gestures, sound sorts, and segmenting.

TABLE 2.4

HIGH-LEVERAGE INSTRUCTIONAL ROUTINES
FOR PHONEMIC AWARENESS

The What: *Routine*	The Why: *Purpose*	The How: *Examples*
"Let's notice how sounds are made." (articulatory gestures)	To provide children a chance to explore how their mouths, lips, tongue, vocal chords, and air flow are used to make different phonemes	"Let's look in the mirror and see what our mouths look like when we make the sound /mmm/."
"Let's put sounds together to make whole words." (blending)	To provide children an entry into phoneme-level work as they listen to a string of separated phonemes and blend them together into a single word	"Listen to the sounds and try to figure out the secret word." /th/-/i/-/k/ = thick /f/-/r/-/ŏ/-/g/ = frog
"Let's take words apart." (segmentation)	To provide children an entry into phoneme-level work as they practice segmenting words of various lengths into their individual phonemes	"You can practice breaking words apart into all of their sounds by talking like a robot." thick = /th/-/ĭ/-/k/ frog = /f/-/r/-/ŏ/-/g/
"Let's listen for sounds that are the same." (isolation and discrimination)	To provide practice noticing how a phoneme in a particular place in one word is the same or different from the phoneme in the same place another word	"Which word doesn't have the same ending (beginning, middle) sound as the others?" bat, cut, bun
"Let's take sounds off of words." (deletion)	To provide practice deleting phonemes from words (This skill is an important prerequisite for the more complex work of phoneme substitution.)	"I'm going to say a word. Then you try to say it back, but don't say the beginning (ending) sound." cat = /ăt/ jump = /ŭmp/

continues

2

The What: *Routine*	The Why: *Purpose*	The How: *Examples*
"Let's change one sound in a word to make a new word." (substitution)	To provide practice with sound substitution (Ultimately, substitution draws on segmenting, deleting, adding, and blending in one task.) Note: Once children have some sound-symbol associations, adding graphemes can actually make substitution more accessible for many children.	"Say *cat*. Now change the /k/ to /m/. What's the new word?" **mat** "Say *mat*. Now change the last sound to /n/. What's the new word?" **man** "Say *man*. Now change the middle sound from /ă/ to /ē/. What's the new word?" **men**

Zooming in on Articulatory Gestures

Thinking about where a phoneme is made in the mouth, or *placement of articulation,* can help children distinguish and remember the sound. It can be helpful to give children mirrors to hold, so they can watch the way their face, mouth, lips, and tongue contribute to making phonemes. Children can even stretch out a whole word, exaggerating its phonemes and noticing the ways the placement of articulation changes. They can also compare phonemes that have similar placement, or phonemes that have very different placements, with each other. Table 2.5 lists sounds and their placement of articulation.

TABLE 2.5

PHONEMES AND PLACEMENT OF ARTICULATION

We Make These Sounds ...	By ...
/p/, /b/, /m/	Putting our lips together
/f/, /v/	Putting our top teeth against our bottom lip
/th/	Putting our tongue between our teeth
/t/, /d/, /n/, /s/, /z/, /l/	Pressing our tongue to the roof of our mouths, just behind the teeth

We Make These Sounds ...	By ...
/j/, /sh/, /ch/	Pressing our tongue on the roof of our mouths, back a bit
/k/, /g/, /ng/	Pressing our tongue to the roof of the mouth, at the back
/ă/, /h/	Opening our throat and mouth
Try it yourself: What do you notice about the placement of articulation for these phonemes? /r/ and /ĭ/	

Adapted from Moats and Tolman 2019

Importantly, some phonemes can be held out for as long as we can support them with our breath. They are referred to as *continuous sounds.* Others are produced by a single puff of air. They are called *stop sounds.* The distinction between these two types of phonemes is important to understand because it affects the way we blend them (more on that in Chapter 3). Table 2.6 offers stop and continuous sounds for you to explore.

TABLE 2.6

STOP AND CONTINUOUS PHONEMES

Some Phonemes ...	For Example ...	They Are Called ...
Are made with one short burst of sound	/b/, /p/, /d/, /t/, /k/, /g/	Stop sounds
Can be held until our breath runs out	/fff/, /mmm/, /nnn/, /sss/, /rrr/, /vvv/, /sh/, /ththth/, /āāā/, /ŏŏŏ/	Continuous sounds
Try it yourself: Which of these phonemes is continuous? Stop? /l/ and /ch/		

It can also be helpful to show children how to place their hands on their vocal chords to feel which phonemes are made with their vocal chords, *voiced,* and which are made with just air, *unvoiced.* Children can feel the vocal cords vibrate on sounds that are voiced. Table 2.7 offers pairs of phonemes that are similar in placement of articulation, even though one is voiced and the other is unvoiced.

TABLE 2.7

VOICED AND UNVOICED PHONEMES

Voiced Phonemes	Unvoiced Phonemes
/b/ (as in bat)	/p/ (as in pie)
/d/(as in duck)	/t/ (as in tent)
/g/ (as in golf)	/k/(as in kiss)
/v/(as in vet)	/f/(as in fish)
/th/ (as in these)	/th/ (as in thin)
zh (as in measure)	/sh/ (as in ship)
Try it yourself: Which of these phonemes is voiced? Unvoiced? /j/ (as in jam) and /ch/ (as in chair)	

Articulatory gestures are complex, and an extensive elaboration on them is beyond the scope of this book. For a deep dive into using articulatory gestures to help children hear phonemes, refer to the work of Louisa Moats and Carol Tolman (2019).

Zooming In on Isolating with Sound Sorts

Sound sorts require students to locate, isolate, and compare the phoneme in a certain position in one word with the phoneme in the same position in another word. Table 2.8 shows how to do a sound sort using two key picture cards.

TABLE 2.8

SOUND SORTS USING PICTURE CARDS

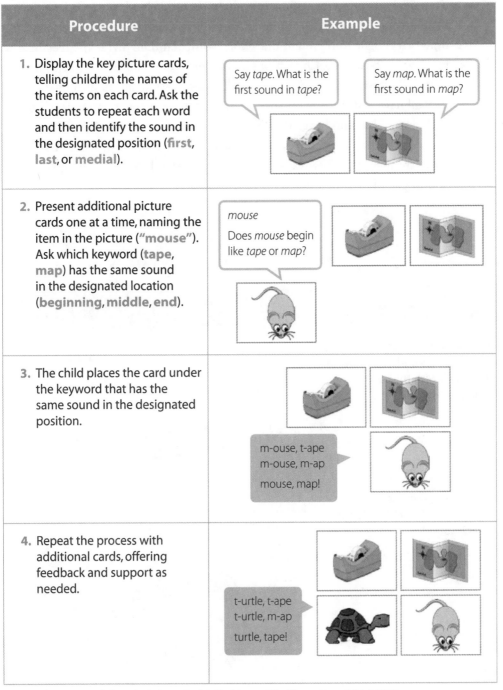

Procedure	Example
1. Display the key picture cards, telling children the names of the items on each card. Ask the students to repeat each word and then identify the sound in the designated position (**first**, **last**, or **medial**).	Say *tape*. What is the first sound in *tape*? Say *map*. What is the first sound in *map*?
2. Present additional picture cards one at a time, naming the item in the picture (**"mouse"**). Ask which keyword (**tape**, **map**) has the same sound in the designated location (**beginning**, **middle**, **end**).	*mouse* Does *mouse* begin like *tape* or *map*?
3. The child places the card under the keyword that has the same sound in the designated position.	m-ouse, t-ape m-ouse, m-ap mouse, map!
4. Repeat the process with additional cards, offering feedback and support as needed.	t-urtle, t-ape t-urtle, m-ap turtle, tape!

Shifting the Balance by Jan Burkins and Kari Yates. Copyright © 2021.

2

 ## Zooming In on Segmenting with Elkonin Boxes

Elkonin boxes (Elkonin 1973) are a versatile and vital scaffold for the complex work of phoneme segmentation. Elkonin boxes make the abstract work of phoneme manipulation visual and multisensory. To make Elkonin boxes, simply draw a rectangle to represent the whole word, and then divide the rectangle into enough boxes for each *phoneme* in the word. For example, words like *sheep*, *goat*, and *cat* would all need three boxes because, despite the number of letters, they all have just three phonemes. In Table 2.9, we share an example of how you can use Elkonin boxes to help students learn to segment the phonemes in a word as they push chips, and eventually letters, into the boxes. Of course, there are many of other ways you can use Elkonin boxes, including simple pointing, and even writing, in the boxes.

TABLE 2.9

SOUND SEGMENTING USING ELKONIN BOXES

Procedure	Example
1. Gather bingo chips or other markers that fit in the boxes and a list of words or picture cards with the desired number of phonemes.	
2. Say the word to be segmented and ask the child to push a chip into the box for each sound.	Push one chip into a box for each sound you hear in the word *chick*. /ch/ – /i/ – /k/

Procedure	Example
3. Once a child has mastered pushing chips into boxes, you can introduce letter manipulatives for simple VC (**am**, **it**) and CVC (**cat**, **run**, **sip**) words. Ask the child to use the letters to push the sounds out of the box. This solidifies the basic tenet of alphabetic principle—sounds are represented by letters, and letters represent sounds.	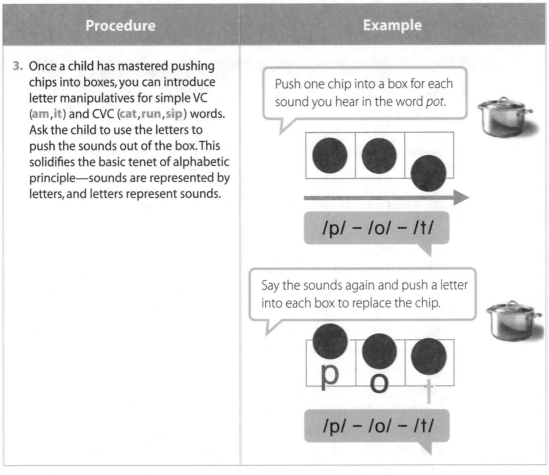

Shifting the Balance by Jan Burkins and Kari Yates. Copyright © 2021.

Get Intentional with Your Instructional Language

There are two ways that our instructional language can actually make developing phonemic awareness harder for children. First, without meaning to, we sometimes use the terms *sounds* and *letters* interchangeably, which can confuse young children. When working to help children learn to hear and manipulate the sounds in language, it's important that we call them just that—*sounds*—or even phonemes. Table 2.10 illustrates some of the ways we can inadvertently confuse the terms *sounds* and *letters*.

TABLE 2.10

COMMON MISTAKES WITH THE TERMS *SOUNDS* AND *LETTERS*

Instead of Saying ...	Say ...
"Listen to the letters in *pin*."	"Listen to the sounds in *pin*."
"What letter do you hear at the beginning of *pin*?"	"What sound do you hear at the beginning of *pin*?"
"How many letters do you hear in the word *pin*?"	"How many sounds do you hear in the word *pin*?"

Being intentional about clean pronunciation of every phoneme during phonemic awareness instruction is *also* critical. Stop sounds (e.g., /p/, /b/, /k/) are especially vulnerable to distorted pronunciations. Sometimes in our eagerness to pronounce these phonemes, we add a breathy "uh," referred to as a *schwa*, to them—turning /b/, for example, into /bŭh/ or /t/ to /tŭh/. Of course, children will pronounce the sounds the way we do, including our mispronunciations! This can cause unnecessary confusion for students.

Here's a hint for clean sound pronunciation of these tricky phonemes. Before making the sound, exhale. Then think, "quick and quiet" as you produce the phoneme. This will help minimize the addition of an extra vowel sound. To watch a video for letter-by-letter rehearsal of phoneme pronunciation, visit **TheSixShifts.com.**

Embed phonemic awareness instruction across the day.

Your students will benefit from a few short phonemic-awareness practice periods spread across the day. To accomplish this, plan for a mix of whole-group instruction and small-group instruction, as well as making use of transition times. Since many of the tasks in Table 2.4 are purely auditory tasks, children can practice them without any materials. For example:

▲ During morning greeting, have children clap the syllables or segment the phonemes in each other's names.

▲ Use Elkonin boxes during interactive writing or in conferences during writing workshop.

▲ While waiting for children to join you on the carpet, play a few quick
   rounds of "Guess My Secret Word," saying the segmented phonemes of
   a word and having children blend them to figure out the secret word.

Let assessment guide you.

You are probably already in the habit of collecting informal data about children's
literacy progress, including letter names, letter sounds, concepts about print,
text reading, and comprehension. But to ensure that every student is developing
phonemic awareness alongside early print skills, you may need to add phonemic
awareness to your ongoing assessment plan. These formative assessment data
are easy to collect during conferences or small-group interactions with students.
Table 2.11 provides a range of options for phonemic awareness assessment.

TABLE 2.11

PHONEMIC AWARENESS ASSESSMENT OPTIONS

Assessment	Description
General observational assessment	Make a table with students' names down the left and columns for phonemic awareness skills across the top. Columns may include categories such as isolationg the initial phoneme, blending two or three phonemes, segmenting two or three phonemes, and so on. Keep the tool close at hand during whole-group and small-group instruction to jot notes on the run.
Individual student progress record for phonemic awareness	You can use Figure 2.5 to keep track of the phonemic awareness progress of individual students, gathering information from either informal observation or more formal practice sessions. Simply make a check mark each time you see the child demonstrate the skill or, for a more precise record, enter the date of the observation.
Homegrown assessment	You can create your own, common formative assessment for phonemic awareness, using the tools and explanations we've provided here.
Formal assessments	There are a variety of phonemic awareness assessment tools on the market. Your school may even already have an assessment tool that includes a phonemic awareness section. You can take a fresh look at what you already have available and how you can utilize it to inform instruction.

Student: **Marissa**

Skills Progression Leading to Phonemic Awareness Proficiency			NOTICE		MANIPULATE	
			Blend	Segment	Add/ Delete	Substitute
STEPPING-STONE SKILLS for Building Phonological Sensitivity **(PREK–EARLY K)**	Smaller and Smaller Segments of Language	Words				
		Compound Words				
		Syllables				
		Onset-rime	✓			✓
POWER SKILLS for Phonemic Proficiency **(K AND BEYOND)**		2 Phonemes	✓✓	✓✓	✓	✓
		3 + Phonemes	✓	✓		
		Words with Blends				

As Needed

ESSENTIAL

Increasingly Complex Manipulations

Shifting the Balance by Jan Burkins and Kari Yates. Copyright © 2021.

FIGURE 2.5 Individual Student Progress Record for Phonemic Awareness

Use the formative assessment data you collect to choose just-in-time practice opportunities for large- and small-group instruction as well as for individual students. As a general rule of thumb, if about half or more of the class is not showing mastery of a skill, whole-group instruction will be most efficient. If ten or fewer students need support with a skill, it's likely that small groups will be more efficient.

Meanwhile, Back in the Classroom . . .

Prompted by their January phonemic awareness data, Ms. Martin and her team decided to zoom in on the phonemic awareness instruction during the winter months. Using a quick formative assessment designed by the group, Ms. Martin was able to confirm that many of her students indeed needed the phonemic awareness support suggested by the formal district measure, especially with regard to segmentation. And with the new measure, she was able to dig a bit deeper, finding out which specific skills were secure for *most*, *some*, or only *a few* of her students.

Ms. Martin is already in the habit of collecting early alphabet knowledge (letter name and letter sound) and concepts about print data during small-group instruction. So, the assessment felt like a relatively simple but powerful addition to her data-collection routine.

She also embedded some new routines into her daily schedule—not one giant block of phonemic awareness drill, but four short but intense bursts of practice aligned with the data she is gathering.

First, during their morning meeting each day, students play "Guess My Secret Word!" In the beginning Ms. Martin offered the segmented sounds and students practiced blending them, but now students are excited to choose and segment their own words, saying them slowly for a partner. The children don't think of this as instruction—they are just having fun. And what is fun for Ms. Martin is that they are beginning to hear the sounds in the middle of words. Next, as the students walk to lunch each day, they quietly tap out the phonemes in cafeteria menu items, as Ms. Martin calls them out—*peas*, *bread*, *milk*, *pizza*. Finally, as a warm-up to phonics instruction each day, students engage in a few minutes of playful practice with a variety of skills.

Ms. Martin has also begun to weave targeted phonemic awareness practice into her small-group instruction. This allows for differentiation, up close assessment, and the opportunity to provide timely personalized feedback. For instance, Ms. Martin may have one group focused on simple sound sorts ("Does *nose* have the same beginning sound as *man* or as *nest*?"). Another group may listen for the subtle differences between medial-vowel phonemes ("Does *bed* have the same middle sound as *pan* or as *pen*?"). A third group may make and break words using magnetic letters ("Make the word *cat*. Now change *cat* to *hat*. Change *hat* to *mat* . . .").

As the school year draws to a close, Ms. Martin is eager to see how her students perform on the district's phonemic awareness measure this time.

Questions for Reflection

Checking In with Yourself: Which of the misunderstandings about phonemic awareness did you find yourself thinking most deeply about? As you work to get intentional about your phonemic awareness instruction, what might your next step be?

High-Leverage Instructional Routines: Which of the phonemic awareness routines are you already using with intentionality? Which of them will you become more intentional about utilizing?

Embedded Throughout the Day: As you reflect on your instructional day, which key routines can you leverage as a regular opportunity for additional phonemic awareness practice?

Task Difficulty: How are you considering articulatory gestures, word complexity, and the phoneme position within words as you plan for phonemic awareness instruction?

Instructional Models: How will you use a thoughtful combination of both whole-group and small-group instruction to differentiate instruction?

Instructional Language: What are you noticing about your instructional language? Are there patterns that are hard to break? What opportunities have you found to be increasingly intentional about phoneme pronunciation?

Differentiation: Who do your current practices best serve? How do you know? Who needs more intentional support?

Formative Assessment: Do you know how well individual students can pronounce, locate, and manipulate individual phonemes in words, including phonemes in different locations within words? What do you need to do to establish or refine your simple formative assessment measures of phonemic awareness?

Reimagining the Way We Teach Phonics

Ms. Lin gathers her first graders on the carpet for the first in a series of phonics lessons on consonant digraphs. She begins by writing *CH* on the board. "Children, this week we are going to be learning about special sounds called digraphs. Digraphs are two letters that make one sound together. Today we are learning the digraph *ch-*. *C* and *H* together make the /ch/ sound. Let's all practice making that sound now. While I point to the letters, you make the sound." The children chant the sound repeatedly as Ms. Lin writes *ch-* over and over again in a column on the board.

Next, Ms. Lin pulls out a paper bag filled with items that start with either *ch-* or other consonant sounds—a *shoe*, a bag of *chips*, a chair from her daughter's doll house, a stapler, a toy truck. The children take turns pulling an item from the bag, and the class helps her decide whether to add the name of each item to the *ch-* list or not.

Next, she asks, "Who can think of another word that has the /ch/ sound in it?" A few students raise their hands. Sonia offers the word *chili*. Victor suggests *Cheerios*. Ms. Lin writes their words on the board. Next, Moesha is excited to remind the class that Christa's name starts with *Ch-*. Ms. Lin points out that, unfortunately, the *ch-* in Christa's name doesn't really follow the "rule"—instead it has the /k/ sound. Ms. Lin then says, "I'm thinking of one more word that starts with *ch-* and is a word that describes some of my favorite people. Watch while I write it."

As the word *children* unfolds on the board, a few children figure it out. Ms. Lin prompts the students to read all the *ch-* words collected on the board. As they do, she notices that many of the children are not able to read these particular words, even though they may now know the beginning digraph. She ends her lesson by reminding the children,

"Remember, whenever you are reading and writing *C* and *H* together, make the /ch/ sound. Say it one more time. What sound?" the children all chant /ch/, as Christa pipes up, "but not in my name!"

Later, at the small-group reading table, Ms. Lin works with a group in a level D text. After thinking about her morning phonics lesson, she is curious to see what students will do when they encounter the newly learned consonant digraph in print. Today's text is about helping with *chores* around the house. But Ms. Lin is disappointed to realize that after the title page, the only opportunities to practice the target digraph *ch-* is on page 6, where the word *chop* appears.

The text *does* include opportunities for students to tackle several consonant blends (*sink, fold, last, find*) they've been practicing over the previous two weeks, but disappointingly, several of the students struggle to read these blends in the connected text.

As her children transition to music, Ms. Lin recognizes familiar but nagging concerns about her phonics instruction. Some students appear to be less engaged week by week, and there seems to be a disconnect between her whole-group phonics instruction and students' application of phonics principles during guided and independent reading. She realizes she is not really even sure who knows which of the phonics patterns she's been teaching and who doesn't. Seeking clarity, she decides to check in with a trusted colleague.

A COMMON PRACTICE TO RECONSIDER

▼ ▼ ▲ ▼ ▼ ▼

Settling for a leave-too-much-to-chance approach to phonics instruction.

Phonics seems to always be a hot button topic. Perhaps, like Ms. Lin, you have experienced a sense that there may be more you can do to elevate your phonics instruction and better meet the needs of your students. Concerned about rigid implementation, phonics program drudgery, and even word calling, many balanced literacy educators are cautious about giving phonics too much instructional real estate. However, in an understandable effort to avoid the risks of isolated skills practice, in many cases we may have overcorrected, and doing so has left a bit too much to chance.

Clearing Up Some Confusion

Given the way the brain reads, the complexities of our alphabetic system, and the amount of practice students need to learn to read, it is worth mustering the courage to look for opportunities to better leverage phonics instruction. After all, one important purpose of phonics instruction is to develop the brain's orthographic processing system, bringing letters, sounds, meaning, and context together. (See Shift 1.)

So, let's take a look at some common misunderstandings about phonics instruction and the reasons we might want to rethink them.

MISUNDERSTANDING:

Learning to recognize letters is just like learning to recognize any other object.

One thing our visual system is naturally good at is recognizing three-dimensional objects—a car, a Lego, a puppy—from any direction. So even if the puppy is lying on its back, our brains know that it is a puppy. And whether the car is driving toward us or away from us, our visual system still recognizes it as a car. But to learn to read, we must actually "unlearn" this *mirror invariance* (Dehaene et al. 2010) because letters work differently.

The reading brain must literally learn to look at letters in a whole new way, recognizing that a stick and a ball is one letter when it faces in one direction—*b*—but when it spins around or flips over, unlike the puppy, it becomes something else altogether—*d*, *p*, or even *q*.

Not only does the reading brain need to look at these special "objects" (letter) differently, it also stores the memory of them differently. This includes carving out a specialized space—think of it as a room in the brain—to store and organize all this new orthographic input. Experts call this space the *visual word form area* (Cohen et al. 2000; Dehaene 2013).

This new way of seeing and storing visual information partly explains why, for so many children, *X* and *O*, with their lovely symmetry, are easy first letters to learn. It also helps us understand that when young children write letters, or even whole words, backward or upside down, its because their brains just haven't completely "unlearned" the other way of seeing.

Helping children learn to suspend mirror invariance when they look at letters can be slow, brain-rewiring work. This challenge is one reason it is extra important that we stock our early literacy classrooms with three-dimensional letters for children to manipulate, avoid teaching visually similar letters close together, and give students lots of practice visually discriminating letter.

MISUNDERSTANDING:

Strengthening phonics instruction means purchasing a program.

Every school needs a program of phonics instruction. But that doesn't necessarily mean you have to buy one. What really matters is a strong and research-informed scope (what will you teach) and sequence (what order you will teach it), alongside solid instructional routines (how you will teach), whether homegrown or purchased ([NRP] 2000; Moats and Tolman 2019). This plan for how phonics instruction will unfold is more than a checklist to ensure "everything gets covered." It actually provides an organizational structure for the brain (Mesmer 2019).

Orthographic knowledge enters the brain like "stuff" enters a child's bedroom. A systematic scope and sequence is to the brain—specifically the visual word form area—what a thoughtful organizational system is to a child's bedroom, with labeled drawers or baskets for everything from socks and pajamas to action figures and art supplies. Organized storage means easier retrieval, for bedrooms and for brains. After all, that Spiderman figure—or letter pattern—is of no use if you can't find it when you want it.

Here are a few brain-friendly and common sense design considerations to keep in mind as you create or evaluate your own scope and sequence (Beck and Beck 2013; Blevins 2017; Duke and Mesmer 2018; Mesmer 2019; Share 2004; Moats and Tolman 2019).

1. **Build from simple to complex.** Start with the easiest skills and build from there. For example, teach letters before simple CVC words, and CVC words before longer words with more complex sounds and spellings.

2. **Teach letters in an order that lets you build words quickly.** This means starting with a few consonants and a single vowel that will quickly move students into word-reading opportunities. For example, knowing the letters M, S, T, P, and A will let children read more than twenty words with a short A sound!

3. **Be aware of letters and sounds that are easily confused.**
   If the visual or auditory characteristics of sounds or their spellings
   are similar, then the instruction for them should be spaced apart.
   For example, the letters M and N, or B and P, should not be taught
   one after another, because they look similar and their sounds are
   easy to confuse.

4. **Provide children frequent opportunities to apply new
   learning.** Because your scope and sequence will let children build
   decodable words quickly, think about how you will give them many
   experiences with their new sounds and letter patterns. From shared
   reading to magnetic letters to beginning texts, each encounter with
   new letter patterns is an opportunity for self-teaching, strength-
   ening neural pathways and developing automaticity (Share 1995,
   1999, 2004).

Table 3.1 can serve as a starting point for organizing beginning phonics
instruction and practice. It lays out a sequential path, beginning with single
letters and sounds and ending with multisyllabic words (NRP 2000). Each of
these steps leads to a deepened understanding of the alphabetic principle and
refinement of the child's organizational system for collecting orthographic
knowledge. Use this tool to develop or reflect on your scope and sequence.

TABLE 3.1

SYSTEMATIC PHONICS PROGRESSION: WHY, WHAT, AND WHEN

Why?	What?	When?
Because children need to understand the principle that ...	We provide explicit phonics instruction and practice with ...	Grade
1. Letters represent sounds.	Matching letter sounds with letter symbols **B = /b/, F = /f/**	K

Why?	What?	When?
Because children need to understand the principle that …	We provide explicit phonics instruction and practice with …	Grade
2. There is a predictable relationship between sounds and their symbols.	Blending/segmenting letter sounds to read/write one-syllable CVC words *cat, mom, run, sip*	K
	Reading/writing simple one-syllable words that have consonant beginning blends (CCVC) and final blends (CVCC) *brim, trot, clap, dust*	K/1
3. Sometimes a single sound is represented by more than one letter.	Reading/writing a few common consonant digraphs *sh, ch, th*	1
	Reading/writing simple one-syllable words that contain beginning consonant digraphs (CCVC) and final consonant digraphs (CVCC) *chop, that, wish, math*	1
4. There are predictable patterns that determine vowel sounds.	Reading/writing single-syllable words that end with *e* (CVCe, CCVCe) *tote, mine, jute, trike, shake*	1
	Reading/writing single-syllable words with vowel teams *(rain, seam, boat)* and vowel digraphs *(glue, out)*	1/2
5. When *R* follows a vowel letter, it changes the vowel sound.	Reading/writing *R*-controlled spellings for each vowel sound (VrC, CVrC, VrCC) *art, corn, march*	1/2
6. Longer words are made up of shorter parts (syllables) that can be decoded bit by bit.	Reading/writing multisyllabic words including compounds, prefixes, and suffixes *cupcake, standing, reread*	2

Grade levels represent an approximation of when the majority of readers are likely ready for instruction.

Unfortunately, there is not a solid body of research to tell us specifically which sound spellings to focus on before others—*A* before *O*? *CH* before *SH*? *FL* before *BR*?—within each of the principles listed above. However, learning along a thoughtful scope and sequence, whether built or bought, can help children develop a structure for their brain's orthographic filing system. This efficient storage and retrieval for sound spellings contributes to eventual word recognition automaticity, improving comprehension, making reading meaningful, and even joyful (NRP 2000; Kirsch et al. 2002; Anderson, Wilson, and Fielding 1998; Johnston, McGeown, and Watson, 2012; McArthur and Castles 2017).

MISUNDERSTANDING:

Phonics isn't really worth teaching because English is unpredictable and its spellings are unreliable.

Yes, on the surface, English can seem like a goofy language. Learning to read English is definitely not as simple as learning one consistent sound (phoneme) for each symbol . . . or one consistent spelling (grapheme) for each sound. Even in a simple sentence such as "The city cat licked her chops," we have to navigate three different pronunciations of the letter *C*, and two different spellings for /k/.

Quite obviously, the math of one-to-one sound-symbol connections does not add up for English! English's forty-four-ish phonemes are represented by 200+ letters and letter combinations known as *graphemes*. Table 3.2 illustrates just a few of the ways English phoneme/grapheme correspondences can be complex.

If all this variability seems complicated, it is, especially for children just learning to read. The way that words are spelled—letter patterns—in a particular alphabetic system is referred to as its *orthography*. An orthography that has many ways to spell the same sound, or many sounds for some spellings, is referred to as *deep* (Seymour, Aro, and Erskine 2003). And English's orthography is obviously very deep!

But it's not that the deep orthography of English isn't decodable. In fact, around half of all words in English are *regular*, which means they use only the most common sound spellings (*tree, bank, interesting*). Another 36 percent are regular except for one uncooperative sound spelling—which is usually a vowel (*find, friend, bread*) (Hanna et al. 1986). Many words that don't appear decodable at first glance, such as *catch* and *knife*, turn out to have very reliable sound spellings (kn-, -tch), nonetheless. So, despite the complexity, there *is* a system to English's orthography (Bowers and Bowers 2017; Coltheart et al. 2001; Kessler and Trieman 2001).

Although it would be ridiculous to try to explicitly teach all of the phoneme-grapheme relationships in English, the complexity of our alphabetic system actually makes phonics instruction *more* important, rather than less (Brady 2011; NRP 2000; Rowe 2005; Spencer and Hanley 2004).

TABLE 3.2

SOUND-SPELLING CORRESPONDENCE EXAMPLES

Phoneme	Number of Spellings	Graphemes	Example
/b/	1	b	ball
/f/	4	f ff ph gh	fun puff phone rough
/k/	5	k c ck ch que	kite cat black choir plaque
/ī/	6	i_e i y igh eigh ie	dime kind try high height tie

3

Remember that filing system for the brain? This system also gives readers a structure for sorting less common letter patterns in English's deep orthography, which don't get explicitly taught (Galuschka et al. 2014; Rose 2006). Organizing orthographic knowledge—knowledge of which letters can typically go together (*ing*, *ble*, *ant*, etc.) and which don't (*prx*, *acb*, *brd*, etc.)—begins with explicit instruction but grows as students continue to read and study words on their own (Share 1995, 1999, 2004).

MISUNDERSTANDING:

If you have a strong scope and sequence and solid instructional routines, you have systematic phonics instruction.

If you are following a carefully designed scope and sequence and making phonics instruction clear and explicit through thoughtful instructional routines, it may seem as though you've checked the boxes for systematic phonics instruction.

But in addition to letter-sound knowledge, there are other understandings and skills children must have to actually read. Children must also understand that letters are spoken sounds written down (alphabetic principle), how to blend those sounds and "make the leap" to a known word (set for variability), and how to use those blended words as a bridge back to meaning (Tunmer and Chapman 2012; Dyson et al. 2017; Elbro and de Jong 2017). Without these skills, children can know all their letters and sounds and still not be able to read.

And there's still more to think about. Following a scope and sequence without thoughtful practice, assessment, and review leads to what Wiley Blevins (2017) refers to as an "exposure" rather than a "mastery" approach. He explains,

> When you adopt a "mastery focus," it changes the way you teach, write lessons, and assess a skill. Once a skill is introduced, you are "in it for the long haul" and don't give up until all your students can successfully apply the skill to authentic reading and writing experiences weeks or months after the initial introduction. (203)

So, cumulative instruction means paying attention to present *and* past learning. Yet, too often instruction and assessment are focused only on the "skill of the week," but not on past skills. Although the curriculum map may indicate a one-week focus for many phonics skills, in reality, most children will need much more time than that. Some of them may even need four to six weeks or more to truly master a skill (Blevins 2017).

To adopt an in-it-for-the-long-haul approach to mastery, assessment, like instruction, needs to be systematic, with attention to sequence, cumulativeness, and repetition. Perhaps you are asking, "How is it possible to keep track of who has really learned which phonics skills in a whole class of children?" One of our favorite ways to assess phonics knowledge is to look closely at student writing. Whether you use samples from writing workshop or periodic dictation of words or sentences, formative data from writing samples will give you an authentic glimpse into the skills students have truly mastered. The ability to apply a phonics skill to writing, after all, is evidence of deep understanding (Treiman and Kessler 2014).

Of course, assessment is not valuable in and of itself. The information we gather from students prepares us to circle back, as illustrated in Figure 3.1, and provide more instruction and practice to the students who need it, whether it

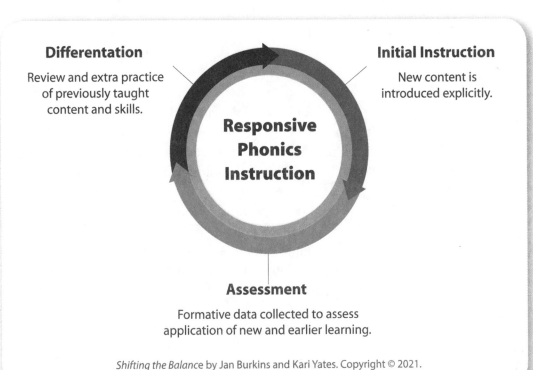

Differentation

Review and extra practice of previously taught content and skills.

Initial Instruction

New content is introduced explicitly.

Responsive Phonics Instruction

Assessment

Formative data collected to assess application of new and earlier learning.

Shifting the Balance by Jan Burkins and Kari Yates. Copyright © 2021.

FIGURE 3.1 From Instruction to Differentiation

is in whole-group, small-group, or individual instruction (Brady, 2020). In this way, assessment serves as a path to differentiation, and our phonics "program" becomes responsive, which is the heart of any good teaching.

So, systematic phonics instruction is not only a plan for what (scope), when (sequence), and how (instructional routines) to teach, but it is also an intentional plan for ongoing practice, assessment, and reteaching (National Institute of Child Health and Human Development 2000; Ehri et al. 2001).

MISUNDERSTANDING:

Learning phonics is boring.

Of course it's possible for any instruction—phonics included—to be boring. But it doesn't have to be. And just because it might seem tedious to us—as people who have already internalized all of the idiosyncrasies of the code—does not mean it will be for children. Explicit phonics instruction is a commitment to letting kids in on the secrets we know about how symbols and sounds match up to make readable words (Snow and Juel 2005).

Engagement and explicit instruction do not need to be mutually exclusive. The brain is a natural puzzle solver and releases endorphins when we solve a problem (Tik et al. 2018). It loves to find patterns and figure things out, and it *is* wired to reward us for our efforts. So, as children use the secrets we've taught them for cracking bits of the code—noticing, comparing, and applying phonic patterns—their brain can reward them for their efforts (Dweck 2017). And although it is possible to turn phonics into the cliché drudgery that we fear, it is also possible to turn phonics instruction into something enticing and empowering. Written language, after all, with all its orthographic demands, is a truly gratifying puzzle to solve.

The up-front support we provide with beginning to solve the great puzzle of our written code not only sets children up for success in the moment but is also proven to increase reading motivation, reading volume, and confidence down the road (Kirsch et al. 2002; Anderson, Wilson, and Fielding 1988; McArthur and Castles 2017).

A Short Summary of the Science

▲ Phonics instruction develops the brain's orthographic processing system, bringing letters, sounds, meaning, and context together.

▲ English has a deep orthography, which makes it especially important to teach phonics.

▲ Most words in English are either completely regular or have one irregular sound spelling pattern.

▲ Explicit instruction includes *both* a thoughtful scope and sequence *and* a plan for assessment and differentiation that ensures mastery versus exposure.

▲ A cohesive scope and sequence help students store and retrieve their orthographic learning more efficiently.

▲ The alphabetic code is a puzzle, and the brain likes to solve puzzles.

▲ Phonics instruction includes both content (letters, letter patterns, sounds) and processes or understandings (alphabetic principle, phonemic analysis, blending, decoding, and meaning making).

▲ Including both systematic phonics and meaningful interactions with texts leads to the most powerful outcomes for beginning readers.

3

THE SIMPLE AND SCIENTIFICALLY SOUND SHIFT

▼ ▼ ▲ ▼ ▼ ▼

Explicitly and systematically teach the secrets of how to crack the written code.

Recommendations for Making the Shift

Given the many misunderstandings about explicit and systematic phonics instruction, you may be wondering what these theoretical ideas actually look like in classroom application.

In this section, we offer a few practical suggestions to help you align your phonics instruction with what science tells us about how the brain learns to read.

Gather what you need for thoughtful phonics instruction.

Phonics instruction doesn't require a fancy kit or curriculum. But it does require some key elements.

1. **Dedicated time** for whole-group and small-group instruction.

2. **A scope and sequence** that represent a thoughtful progression of skills.

3. **A linking chart and frieze cards** depicting consistent key words for teaching each sound. (Download our Linking Chart and Key Word Cards at **TheSixShifts.com**.)

4. **A robust collection of word lists** representative of each spelling pattern being taught. (Download spelling pattern lists at **TheSixShifts.com**.)

5. A collection of **high-leverage instructional routines** for blending, segmenting, and word building. We offer a few instructional strategies below in Table 3.3 and zoom in on two of them—blending and word building—in the sections that follow.

6. A thoughtful **assessment plan** so that student progress can inform your reteaching and differentiation efforts.

Learn to use a few high-leverage instructional routines.

You don't need a huge number of routines to teach phonics effectively, and you certainly don't need a bunch of worksheets or cute activities. In Table 3.3, we offer a collection of instructional routines that—together with a thoughtful scope and sequence and a plan for differentiation—will position you for strong, systematic instruction. If you use a purchased program, it is our hope that you will recognize these routines as part of what you are already doing or possibly use this as a guide to enhance your practices.

After Table 3.3, we zoom in on blending and building words with word chains.

TABLE 3.3

HIGH-LEVERAGE INSTRUCTIONAL ROUTINES
FOR SYSTEMATIC PHONICS INSTRUCTION

The What: *Routine*	The Why: *Purpose*	The When: *Frequency*
"Let's play with sounds."	To provide ongoing phonemic awareness practice	Daily
"Let's study something new."	To provide explicit instruction and modeling of new phonics skills from scope and sequence	1–3 times per week
"Let's blend some words."	To provide practice reading words that use the pattern being taught as well as a review of past skills/patterns	Daily
"Let's build some words."	To provide practice with building words and changing them to new words, one sound at a time (word chains with minimal contrast)	2–3 times per week
"Let's write some words."	To provide purposeful practice applying newly learned phonics patterns to writing new words	2–3 times per week
"Let's study some spellings."	To provide practice analyzing and writing words with two familiar but contrasting spelling patterns	2–3 times per week
"Let's read!"	To provide opportunities for students to encounter the targeted skills in meaningful contexts (sentences, passages, books)	Daily
"Let's review something that was a little tricky."	To provide additional explicit review, modeling, and practice of previously taught skills	As needed

Zooming In on Blending

Blending is a critical bridge from isolated skills—"I know what sounds the letters make"—to application—"I can use those letter sounds to decode a word." There are two types of blending: continuous and cumulative. To help you understand the difference and see how each type of blending looks in practice, we provide examples below.

Continuous Blending: The continuous blending routine teaches children to move across a word in a linear fashion, saying each sound in order and blending them together. When you think of blending sounds together to decode a word, this routine is likely what comes to mind. Table 3.4 describes each step of modeling this process.

TABLE 3.4

CONTINUOUS BLENDING ROUTINE

Procedure	Example
Write the word, or display letter tiles, letter cards, or magnetic letters that spell the word.	Let's blend this word. **m a t**
Point to each letter or grapheme, pronouncing and holding (as possible) each sound as you move to the next letter.	/mm/ /aa/ /t/ **m a t**
Move your finger back to the beginning of the word and draw your finger under all the letters quickly as you read the word.	/mat/ The word is mat. **mat**

NOTE Remember, continuous sounds, such as those represented by the graphemes *f, l, m*, a, *n*, etc., can be sustained or held, but stop sounds, such as those represented by b, p, d, and h, etc., cannot. Holding continuous sounds minimizes the addition of a schwa to consonant sound pronunciations.

TABLE 3.5

STEPS FOR TEACHING CUMULATIVE BLENDING

Procedure	Example
Display the letter tiles, letter cards, or magnetic letters that spell the word. Leave generous space between each letter.	Let's blend this word. m a t
Point to each of the first two letters, pronouncing their sounds and pausing between them.	/mm/ . . . /ăă/ m a t . .
Physically push the first two letters together and slide your finger under them as you blend the sounds.	/mmăă/ m a t →
Slide your finger under the first two sounds again, blending the sounds as you say them. Then pause while you lift your finger and point to the next sound as you say it separately.	/mm/ăă/ . . . /t/ m a t → .
Physically push the third letter next to the others and slide your finger under them as you blend all three sounds together.	/măt/ mat →
Draw your finger quickly under all three letters as you read the whole word.	/măt/ The word is mat. mat →

Cumulative Blending: Cumulative blending slows the process down even more, breaking it into smaller chunks of work. This method can assist students in overcoming the short-term memory challenges that sometimes interfere with trying to hold onto all the sounds across an entire word. Table 3.5 illustrates each step in this process.

Successful blending is the bridge from the isolated skill work of phonics back to meaningful language, so get your students blending from the very beginning. Students don't have to know every letter sound to get started. With even just a handful of consonant letters (*M, S, T, P*) and a single vowel letter (*A*), students can begin to blend sounds to make words (*at, am, mat, pat, tap, sat, sap*). As children become more fluent and begin to recognize familiar orthographic patterns—blends, digraphs, inflectional endings, etc.—their accumulated blending efforts pay off, and they become more efficient.

Zooming In on Building Words with Word Chains

One of the most powerful ways to help students deepen their phonics *and* phonemic awareness skills simultaneously is through word-building activities, also known "word chains" or "making and breaking words." Children practice this routine with letter cards, letter tiles, or our favorite—three-dimensional magnetic letters. Word-building practice can take place in whole-group, small-group, or one-on-one instructional settings and can be adapted for any phonics skill that students need to practice.

To get started, you need a list of about five to eight words that match the focus of your instruction. Each word should vary by only one sound (minimal contrast). Next, you'll give students the letters that are required to make *all* of the words in the series. And finally, let students know which word to make first, next, and so on. There are two general variations of this routine.

▲ **Routine 1: What's the New Word?**

This process is the simpler of the two variations. Here, the teacher tells students what specific letters to use to make a word. The primary job of the students is to use blending to figure out each new word.

▲ **Routine 2: What Will You Change?**

In this variation, the teacher tells the student what word to make and the student must decide which letters to use for the initial word. Then, for each subsequent word, the child trades out the letter that needs to change. This more-challenging version of word building requires phoneme manipulation, including segmenting, deleting, and substitution.

Table 3.6 includes language and a sequence of words for both word-building routines.

TABLE 3.6

TWO VARIATIONS OF WORD CHAINS

Routine 1: *What's the New Word?* (Simpler)	Routine 2: *What Will You Change?* (Harder)	Chain
"Use the letters *c, a, t* to spell your first word." "What is the word?"	"Which letters will you need to spell the word *cat*?" "Read the word."	cat
"Now change the *c* to *h*." "What's the new word?"	"Now make it say *hat*." "What will you change?"	hat
"Now change the *t* to *m*." "What's the new word?"	"Now make it say *ham*." "What will you change?"	ham
"Now change the *h* to *r*." "What's the new word?"	"Now make it say *ram*." "What will you change?"	ram
"Now change the *m* to *p*." "What's the new word?"	"Now make it say *rap*." "What will you change?"	rap

You can make word-building activities simpler or more complex based on the needs of your students. Table 3.7 shows examples of word chains with increasing levels of complexity. For a complete progression of word chain lists to support readers in each of the stages of early reading, go to **TheSixShifts.com**.

TABLE 3.7

EXAMPLES OF WORD CHAINS WITH INCREASING COMPLEXITY

Phonetic Skill Focus	Example Word Chain Sequences
Changes to only beginning consonant	cat →hat →bat →mat →fat →rat
Changes to beginning and ending consonant	cat →cap →map →mat →man
Changes to medial vowel	rid →rod →red →rad
Changes to initial consonant blends and medial vowel	sap →slap →slip →-lip →nip →nap →snap
Alternating between simple initial consonant and initial consonant digraph	cat →chat →-hat →that
Changes to initial consonant, final consonant digraph, and medial vowel	math →mash →cash →dash →dish →with →wish
Alternating between short vowel (CVC) and long vowel (CVCe)	cap →cape →-ape →tape →tap- →tab →tub →tube

Let assessment guide you.

Chances are you already have access to more phonics assessments than you have time to make use of. Systematic phonics instruction requires systematic reflection on student progress. The trick is figuring out which assessments will give you the most and best information about your students, without taking up too much time. So, you will want to be very selective. Here are a few things to consider as you decide which assessments to use with students:

▲ **Whole-Class Versus Individual Administration**

Whole-class administration will give you more information in less time, and individual assessments will give you an opportunity to watch each child work up close.

▲ **In Context Versus in Isolation**

In-context assessments, such as running records, show how children utilize phonics on the run and with the support of context for cross-checking. Assessments of phonics skills in isolation let you zoom in on specific sequential skills.

▲ **Real Words Versus Pseudowords**

Assessments of real words in isolation will give you information about how well children can problem solve words using orthographics and meaning but without context. Assessing pseudowords lets you focus just on orthographic knowledge, because it lets you see what children do with a completely novel word.

▲ **Reading Versus Writing**

Reading assessments let you see how well children can decode, and writing assessments let you see how well children can encode.

In Table 3.8, we offer some examples of words and sentences that you can use as quick informal assessments of students' ability to read or write words with each of the phonetic concepts. These cumulative reading (decoding) and writing (encoding) prompts align to the progression of phonics knowledge in Table 3.1 and can help you see which of the categories of orthographic learning is already within the student's grasp and which needs more attention.

TABLE 3.8

SAMPLE WORDS AND SENTENCES FOR INFORMAL ASSESSMENT

Orthographic Learning (File Drawer)	Sample Words for Decoding or Encoding	Sample Sentences for Decoding or Encoding
Simple short vowel sound spellings **(VC, CVC)**	*sad, bet, rib, hop, sum*	Jen has a pup in a box.
Beginning and final consonant blends **(CCVC, CVCC)**	*swam, slop, club, brim, help, wing, plump*	We went on a trip past a frog pond.
Beginning and final consonant digraphs **(CCVC, CVCC)**	*ship, mash, chop, such, thin, math, sick*	Seth has a rash on his chin.
Long vowel sound spellings created by final *e* **(CVCe, CCVCe)**	*shake, pine, lobe, fuse, Pete*	Is it safe to bike to the cove with Luke?
Vowel team sound spellings and vowel digraphs	*train, beam, roast, pie, mouth, grew*	Rain blew in the boat, and his boots and feet got wet.
R-controlled vowel sounds	*harm, term, shirt, port, lurk*	Her car will turn at the barn and go north.

(You can access more words and sentences like these, as well as tools for keeping track of individual student progress, at **TheSixShifts.com**.)

As students read or write these or other words and sentences, think of their "mistakes" as opportunities to see their thinking. The trick is to view reading miscues or spelling errors as formative data about what students *do* know. This important glimpse into the growing orthographic knowledge they have (and have not) internalized can help you take an in-it-for-the-long-haul approach to phonics instruction.

Meanwhile, Back in the Classroom . . .

For a long time, Ms. Lin has worried that when it comes to application of phonics, her kids were all over the map. To her, the content and order of the district pacing guide seem strong, but she's realized she needs to slow things down, become more aware of which of her students control which phonics skills, and differentiate her instruction more deliberately.

Modeling her own word lists after a colleague's, Ms. Lin has begun to administer a quick spelling dictation assessment at the conclusion of each week's phonics instruction. Because each week's five words, which students don't study beforehand, are dictated to the whole class at once, the assessment takes only a few minutes. Each list contains three words with the most recently taught sound spellings and two review words. For instance, last week's five words—*bone*, *flake*, *choke*, *crash*, *land*—allowed her to reflect not only on students' mastery of the CVCe pattern (this week's skill) but also on children's proficiency with short vowel words ending in a blend or consonant digraph.

Skeptical at first, Ms. Lin has been surprised by how informative this simple spelling measure has been, and how much *last* Friday's assessment shaped her planning for phonics instruction *this* week. The assessment confirmed that, contrary to what the pacing guide recommends, her students need another week to review and practice reading and writing CVCe words.

On Monday, she gives students whiteboards and engages children in a familiar process of making and labeling a T-chart. "Let's listen to and write some words," she begins. "At the top of your board, write *cap* and *cape*. When I say a word, you can decide if it has a spelling pattern like cap or a spelling pattern like cape."

As she says each word for students to consider, she reminds them to compare the new words to the key words at the top of their chart.

cap	cape
rob	robe
dim	rate
rat	fine

As she watches the children write the words in the columns, it is easy to see that several children need additional practice, and she makes notes on her clipboard. She will provide these students a few minutes of word building during small-group instruction—where managing magnetic letters is more practical and she can scaffold their practice with immediate feedback—before they dig into beginning reading texts, which will give them additional practice with CVCe words in context.

Finally, during interactive writing, Ms. Lin sneaks in some authentic practice of CVCe words. She tells the students (a mostly true) tale of a recent bike ride. Together they construct and write "Ms. Lin rode her bike to the lake. She saw a snake along the path. Yikes!"

Questions for Reflection

Checking In with Yourself: Which of the misunderstandings about phonics instruction did you find most thought-provoking? Which ones have you believed and how has your thinking changed? How will your phonics instruction change as a result?

Dedicated Time: How much dedicated time do you have in your schedule for whole-group and small-group phonics instruction? Is it enough to allow a truly explicit and systematic approach and teach to mastery?

Scope and Sequence: Have you adopted or developed a thoughtful, multigrade progression of skills that honors the six principles in Table 3.1 on page 68–69?

Instructional Routines: With which high-leverage instructional routines for blending, segmenting, and word building are you most comfortable? Which do you want to practice or explore further?

Program Evaluation: If you are following a program, what is your plan for evaluating its instructional progression as well as any routines it recommends, revising them as necessary?

Formative Assessment: Have you gathered formative assessment tools, such as word lists and sentences for dictation? What phonics assessments are already at your disposal? What combination of them offers you the most complete and helpful information about your students?

Differentiation: Who do your current practices best serve? Who will benefit the most from a shift in practice? What next steps will you take to inform your reteaching and differentiation?

Revisiting High-Frequency Word Instruction

Ms. Ellis has gathered a group of six first graders around a kidney-shaped table to tackle some word work before sharing a guided reading text.

She wants to give them specific practice with the word *does* because she knows they will encounter it multiple times in today's new book, *What Does an Animal Do?* She writes does on a dry erase board saying each letter in the word aloud as she writes it and then pronounces the whole word with a bit of flair as she finishes. "This is one of our heart words," she explains. "You can't sound it out. You have to just know it by heart."

The children nod. This is familiar information.

Ms. Ellis names and points to each letter in the word *does* and then reads the word aloud. She repeats this process a few times, asking the children to join in with her.

Next, Ms. Ellis erases the word, and asks the children to write *does* on their individual dry erase boards.

The children all write the word *does* successfully, except for Jon, who has some trouble and ends up writing, *duz*. Ms. Ellis corrects his mistake by calling out the correct letters and letting him compare what she is saying with what he has written. Jon finds and fixes his error.

Once Ms. Ellis has checked their spelling, the students begin their familiar routine, repeatedly chanting the letters in *does* and reading the word, *"D-o-e-s, does! D-o-e-s, does! D-o-e-s, does!"* This continues for a minute or so, with the children pointing to each letter as they say it and then briskly running their fingers under the whole word as they chant the culminating *"does!"* Finally, they erase the word and write it again from memory, saying the letters as they write each one.

Confident that the children now know the word *does*, Ms. Ellis passes out the new text, which the students are clearly excited to dig into. After an introduction and a brief picture walk, they begin reading. Alex reads the first few pages but gets stuck on a word on page 2. She looks at her teacher and back at the word.

On what word do you think Alex is stuck?

You guessed it.

Surprisingly (or not surprisingly), Alex is stuck on *does*—the very word she was writing, spelling, and reading correctly just a few minutes earlier.

Perhaps this sounds familiar.

A COMMON PRACTICE TO RECONSIDER

▼ ▼ ▼ ▲ ▼ ▼

Taking a "just-have-to-memorize-them" approach to teaching high-frequency words

Most of us have engaged in one process or another—from flash cards to rainbow writing to chanting routines—in an effort to help children commit important words to long-term memory. Unfortunately, most of us also know the disappointment and even the confusion that comes from seeing a student read or write a word in practice one minute and stare blankly at it on the page in the next minute. And, given the irregular spellings, when children are stuck on these words, they are truly stuck (and *frequently*, since they are, after all, high-*frequency* words!).

High-frequency words are the ubiquitous and abstract words that are the glue of spoken language. But in English, the written form of *some* of these words is represented by seemingly unpredictable strings of letters. These *irregular* words present the reader with unexpected silent letters (*should*), rule-breaking vowels (*want*), and consonants that take on surprising roles (*does*).

Because of the unclear connection between the sounds and letters in many of these words, it makes intuitive sense they should be learned "by sight." In fact, most of us have been strongly cautioned against asking children to even *try* to sound out these words. We've been told instead that students just have to "know them."

The way we have always taught sight words *seems* to make good common sense. Nevertheless, this just-have-to-know-them approach leaves students without strategies for figuring them out when they actually *don't* know them. After all, they can't sound them out.

Or can they?

Clearing Up Some Confusion

Important science about how the brain learns to read positions us to rethink some longtime, intuitive assumptions about high-frequency word learning.

Let's take a look at some common misunderstandings and the reasons we might want to rethink them.

 MISUNDERSTANDING:

Sight words are the same as high-frequency words.

Just like all tulips are flowers, but not all flowers are tulips, all high-frequency words *can* be sight words, but not all sight words are high-frequency words.

Sight words can actually be *any* kind of word. They *might* be high-frequency words (*the, was, could*), but they don't have to be. They can also be words that are near and dear to a reader (*ice cream, Grandma,* or *Superman*) or words that show up a lot when someone reads a topic of interest (*geranium, deadhead, horticulture*).

Sight words, referred to as "brain words" by Gentry and Ouellette, are simply all words, not just high-frequency words, that we have come to know through sight, sound, and meaning and have stored away in the visual word form area of the brain for quick retrieval (2019). As an expert reader, almost *every* word you read has become a sight word for you (Adams 1990; Ehri 1995, 1998, 2005a; Kilpatrick 2015). But just because any word can eventually become a sight word doesn't mean that some words don't show up more frequently than others.

High-frequency words—those that show up most frequently in text—are especially important for students to learn. In fact, it seems a bit crazy but thirteen little words account for more than 25 percent of the words in print! And the 109 words in Table 4.1 and their derivatives (i.e., *look, looked, looking, looks*) make up half of all of the words children will encounter while reading

(Adams 1990; Blevins 2017; Carroll, Davies, and Richman 1971). What's more, when equipped with the first 109 words plus some basic phonics knowledge, children can read 90 percent of the single syllable words they encounter in texts (Solity and Vousden 2009).

TABLE 4.1

109 HIGH-FREQUENCY WORDS THAT MAKE UP 50 PERCENT OF WORDS IN CHILDREN'S TEXTS

1	the	19	they	42	their	65	two	88	use
2	of	20	at	43	said	66	like	89	may
3	and	21	be	44	if	67	him	90	water
4	a	22	this	45	do	68	see	91	long
5	to	23	from	46	will	69	time	92	little
6	in	24	I	47	each	70	could	93	very
7	is	25	have	48	about	71	no	94	after
8	you	26	or	49	how	72	make	95	words
9	that	27	by	50	up	73	than	96	called
10	it	28	one	51	out	74	first	97	just
11	he	29	had	52	them	75	been	98	where
12	for	30	not	53	then	76	its	99	most
13	was	31	but	54	she	77	who	100	know
Words 1–13 make up 25 percent of the words in children's texts.		32	what	55	many	78	now	101	get
		33	all	56	some	79	people	102	through
		34	were	57	so	80	my	103	back
		35	when	58	these	81	made	104	much
		36	we	59	would	82	over	105	before
14	on	37	there	60	other	83	did	106	go
15	are	38	can	61	into	84	down	107	good
16	as	39	an	62	has	85	only	108	new
17	with	40	your	63	more	86	way	109	write
18	his	41	which	64	her	87	find		

Adapted from Adams (1990) and Carroll, Davies, and Richmond (1971)

This means that strategic effort helping readers store a few dozen high-frequency words in the word form area of the brain can free up a lot of working memory. Less attention spent on deciphering the words means students can direct more attention toward comprehending the text (Kilpatrick 2015; LaBerge and Samuels 1974).

MISUNDERSTANDING:

High-frequency words can't be decoded.

It is common practice to describe high-frequency words as un-decodable, or *irregular*. But this isn't completely true. Although it *is* true that some high-frequency words are less decodable, or rule-governed, than others, all words have some degree of decodability, even the most irregular ones (Adams 1990; Seidenberg 2017; Castles, Rastle, and Nation 2019). They all have some letters and/or letter strings that are familiar and predictable. Consider the following irregularly spelled high-frequency words. For each word, notice what *is* reliable about the sound spellings within it:

> *are, been, come, could, do, does, done, give, have, live, of,*
> *one, said, some, the, their, they, their, to, was, want, who,*
> *would, you*

Also, most words considered to be irregular actually have patterns that are found in at least a few other words. So although they *are* irregular, or have exceptions to the rules, they are still somewhat consistent (Adams 1990; Seidenberg 2017; Moats and Tolman 2019). For example, learning the sound-to-spelling alignment, or *mapping,* of the word *was* can make it easier for children to learn *want* and *wash*. Learning the sound-to-symbol mapping for *should* can make it easier to learn *would* and *could*.

Furthermore, and of considerable importance, many high-frequency words are absolutely decodable, which makes their assignment to the flash card pile or the word wall unnecessary. Here are just a few examples of completely regular high-frequency words:

> *a, and, big, came, can, down, each, fast, get, how, in, like,*
> *make, not, play, read, see, stop, them, try, went, will, yes*

Because so many high-frequency words are so regular, they may need little specialized instruction at all. So rather than teach these decodable high-frequency words (*can*, *it*, *went*) separately as sight words, we can make learning them even easier by teaching them in connection with our phonics lessons—teaching the word *and* alongside short *a*, *in* alongside short *i*, *get* alongside short *e*, and so on (Suggate 2016; Duke and Mesmer 2018).

But even high-frequency words that *don't* completely follow rules and seem un-decodable have at least some decodability. In connected text especially, children can attempt to sound these words out, just like any word they don't know. The probability of children successfully figuring out an irregularly spelled word by decoding it—and trying to "make the leap" from partial to full decoding with some assistance from meaning and context (set for variability)—tends to be higher than most other options, such as trying to find the word on a classroom word wall.

MISUNDERSTANDING:

Children just need to memorize irregularly spelled high-frequency words as whole units.

One important scientific finding about high-frequency words is that they are not simply learned by sight. And although it may appear on the surface as though proficient readers are recognizing words immediately as whole units, brain research very convincingly refutes this common assumption (Ehri 2005b; Siedenberg 2017; Willingham 2017). In truth, research shows that it is actually the locked-in memories of sounds and their corresponding letter orders that make expert readers *look* as if they have memorized the words. In *Brain Words*, Richard Gentry and Gene Ouellette (2019) explain, "Skilled reading is so efficient that you aren't even aware that you are using these stored *spellings* because it happens in such a seemingly automatic way" (13).

Because our own eyes can move quickly and effortlessly across the page, with our phonological, orthographic, meaning, and context processing systems taking less than a second to make sense of word after word after word, it is easy to intuitively assume we are reading these words as whole units. But we aren't. Even when we know the words automatically, reading them requires scanning the entire sequence of letters, and checking it against sound and meaning (Adams 1990; Gentry and Ouellette 2019). If you weren't processing the individual letters, for instance, you would likely miss the subtle differences between *flap* and *flop*, *inference* and *interference*, *stationary* and *stationery*, or *insulting* and *insulating*. But you don't.

Instead, you recognize the word as a familiar string of letters that have a precise *and* meaningful order, are associated with a particular sound sequence, and carry a certain meaning (Kilpatrick 2016). At some point you learned this order, not just by studying the letters on the page but by doing the mental work of puzzling through how the precise order of the sounds in the word matches, or maps onto, the specific order of the graphemes on the page (Seidenberg 2017). When it comes to learning the subtle differences between often-confused high-frequency words like *the*, *then*, *them*, and *they*, reconciling the way the sounds and the spellings align is critical!

MISUNDERSTANDING:

The best way to learn high-frequency words is to practice reading, writing, and/or chanting the letters over and over.

To learn the meaningful order of the letters in a word (regardless of how regular or irregular the word is) takes more than just reciting the letters in order (*t-h-e-y*), studying the whole word on a flash card, or writing the word ten times in a row—even if the writing is in fun colors or with scented markers. To really learn any new word you have to get in and do some phonemic analysis, comparing the word's sound structure to its spelling. This sound-to-spelling work, known as *orthographic mapping*, is essential, whether the word is very easily decodable (*at*) or irregularly spelled (*should*) (Ehri 2014; Seidenberg 2017).

Taking the spoken word and the written word apart and then matching up the two—phonemes to graphemes—is how the spelling of a word gets locked in long-term memory. This locking in is the magic of orthographic mapping, and it is *speech-to-print* work, as opposed to the *print-to-speech* work of decoding. In other words, the work of learning a word by sight—whether regular or irregular—could actually begin with eyes closed, since you first have to listen to the sounds in a word, even if you are just saying them inside your head.

But because of the deep orthography of English, this alignment work isn't always straightforward. Table 4.2 shows some words for which the work of matching, or mapping, the spoken sounds to the written letters might be tricky, or even counterintuitive.

4

TABLE 4.2

ORTHOGRAPHIC MAPPING EXAMPLES

Word	Taking Apart by Sound (Phonemic Analysis)	Taking Apart by Spelling (Orthographic Analysis)	Alignment (Orthographic Mapping)
they	/th/ /ā/ (2 sounds)	t-h-e-y (4 letters)	/th/ /ā/ th | ey
laugh	/l/ /a/ /f/ (3 sounds)	l-a-u-g-h (5 letters)	/l/ /ă/ /f/ l | au | gh
does	/d/ /ə/ /z/ (3 sounds)	d-o-e-s (4 letters)	/d/ /ə/ /z/ d | oe | s
knight	/n/ /ī / /t/ (3 sounds)	k-n-i-g-h-t (6 letters)	/n/ /ī/ /t/ kn | igh | t

Orthographic mapping helps readers come to know high-frequency words—or any words—automatically. This orthographic mapping process may seem like only a subtle difference from chanting the letters, but it is critical if we want children to move words into the long-term storage of their visual word form area. We offer more guidance on this process in the instructional recommendations at the end of this chapter.

5

MISUNDERSTANDING:

If you can read a word, you know it.

There are lots of ways of thinking about the developmental journey children take as readers, and many researchers have identified phases of development. In fact, you probably already have a familiar model for thinking about how readers and writers grow and change in stages or phases. In Table 4.3, we share a continuum of growth developed by Linnea Ehri (1995, 2002, 2005a, 2017).

What makes these Ehri phases different from others? They zoom in on *word recognition*, describing the increasingly sophisticated ways children read and write words. For example, a child goes from "knowing" the word *stop* by recognizing the context of the red sign to knowing it because it starts with /s/ like a sibling's name, to knowing it because it is decodable letter by letter, to really *knowing* it because opportunities to match its spelling to its sounds (orthographic mapping) have made it automatic.

In each of Ehri's phases, children learn to look at print in new ways. Of course, children don't just jump all at once from one phase to the next, but rather the phases overlap, and children's progress from one to the next will vary.

TABLE 4.3

READING AND WRITING WORDS ACROSS EHRI'S PHASES

Phase	Reading Words	Writing Words
Pre-alphabetic	Looks at the picture on the **library** sign and states, "That says library!"	Draws a picture of a **knight**, writes squiggles and the letters *b f g r* and reads, "The knight is brave."
Partial alphabetic	Looks at the picture and the first letter on the **library** sign and says, "/lll/…That says library!"	Draws a picture of a knight, writes *nT Z Bv*, and reads, "The knight is brave."
Full alphabetic	When encountering the word *library* in text, the reader works across it sequentially, decoding each chunk sound by sound.	Draws a picture of a **knight**, writes *The nite braivlee fot the draygin*, and reads "The knight bravely fought the dragon."
Consolidated	When encountering the word *library* in text, the reader easily recognizes and blends known chunks—*li-bra-ry*.	Because the child has seen *knight* in print and has learned to read and spell *light* and **knife**, the child easily writes **knight**.
Automatic	When encountering the word *library* in text, the reader processes the letters automatically (in a fraction of a second), without the need for problem solving.	Writes words such as **knight**, **shield**, **castle** fluently, drawing easily from a vast mental dictionary of stored words.

Adapted from Ehri (2002)

As Table 4.3 illustrates, on the path to automaticity and fluency, how word reading and writing look different in each phase. Although it is tempting to think that children in the partial or full alphabetic phase "know" the words they can read, until each of the words is automatic, they have not yet become sight words. Remember, *all* words are sight words for proficient readers, and we process every little bit of these words in a fraction of a second (Seidenberg 2017).

But getting to the automatic phase of reading requires deepening *lexical quality*, which is how much a reader knows about a specific word (Perfetti and Hart 2002; Perfetti 2007). For every reader, each word in their total collection of known words is of varying lexical quality; they just know some words better than others (Castles and Nation 2006). Lexical quality grows each time a child notices or learns something more about a word's sound structure, spelling, or meaning. For some children, lexical quality increases quickly, requiring just a few experiences with a word to really know it. Although different researchers have arrived at different conclusions, most agree that it takes ten or less encounters to truly learn a word. Of course, having difficulty with reading can require many, many more (Blevins 2017; Kilpatrick 2015; Reitsma 1983).

So, each encounter with a word that is not yet "high quality" is an opportunity to strengthen neural pathways and anchor the word—its sight, sound, *and meaning*—in memory. Ideally, every word becomes a sight word, resulting in fluent reading and allowing children to direct more and more of their attention to comprehension (Klauda and Guthrie 2008; LaBerge and Samuels 1974), which is the whole point of reading, after all (Ehri 2005b; Perfetti 2007; Willingham 2017).

A Short Summary of the Science

▲ A sight word is any word that the brain recognizes automatically.

▲ High-frequency words are words that are especially high leverage because of how often they are found in written texts.

▲ Knowing as few as 13 of the 109 to most frequently occurring words unlocks 25 to 50 percent of all texts written for children.

▲ Proficient readers don't memorize whole words, even though they look as though they do. They rapidly process every letter in a word.

▲ To establish *any* word as a sight word, anchoring it in the visual word form area requires orthographic mapping.

▲ Orthographic mapping is aligning speech to print. Decoding is aligning print to speech.

▲ Ehri's phases show a predictable progression of development for readers and writers as they move from the pre-alphabetic to the automatic phase of word recognition.

▲ Lexical quality depends on how much phonological, orthographic, meaning, and context knowledge a reader/writer has accumulated about a word, engaging all four processing systems.

▲ Reading and writing fluency varies based on the lexical quality of the words we know, because higher lexical quality makes retrieval of information automatic.

▲ Automatic word recognition frees up attention for comprehension.

4

THE SIMPLE AND SCIENTIFICALLY SOUND SHIFT

▼ ▼ ▼ ▲ ▼ ▼

Create opportunities for children to "pull apart" the phonemes in high-priority words and match each one to the grapheme(s) that represent them.

Recommendations for Making the Shift

If you are wondering what you can do to help children better learn words, especially irregularly spelled, high-frequency words, this section offers suggestions.

These recommendations for supporting students in learning tricky but important words are surprisingly simple. Although a few might feel counterintuitive, they are, nonetheless, scientifically sound.

Learn to use a few high-leverage instructional routines.

Using simple but versatile instructional routines, you can consistently help students move toward automatic word recognition. A few reliable routines, coupled with clear language that supports them, will make both teaching and learning easier. We share a few such routines in Table 4.4, and then zoom in on prioritizing words and orthographic mapping.

TABLE 4.4

HIGH-LEVERAGE INSTRUCTIONAL ROUTINES FOR WORD LEARNING

The What: *Routine*	The Why: *Purpose*	The How: *Examples*
Prioritize high-frequency words for instruction.	To organize high-frequency words for instruction based on urgency, decodability, or alignment to phonics rules	Identify words to teach with short *a*, such as *and*, *at*, *as*, *can*, and *man*.
Focus on phonology.	To model stretching a word, listening for each distinct sound in order, and paying attention to what the mouth, lips, tongue, and air flow are doing (articulatory gestures)	"Let's listen to the sounds in the word *mango*. How many syllables? How many sounds? Say it again with your eyes closed and notice what you do with your mouth and lips."
Connect speech to print through orthographic mapping in and out of context.	To provide an auditory and visual model of the alignment between sounds and symbols using Elkonin (1973) boxes for orthographic mapping.	"Watch while I write the word *people*. Let's match the sounds we hear in the word *people* to its letters. We can write the spelling for each sound in its own box."

continues

The What: *Routine*	The Why: *Purpose*	The How: *Examples*
Strengthen lexical quality.	To deepen lexical quality by reading and writing words in and out of context, connecting phonological, orthographic, meaning, and context knowledge (four-part processing)	"Hey, here's the word *mango* again. Do you remember what a mango is? Let's take another look at the word, thinking again about how its sounds and spelling match up."
Repeated readings	To give students authentic opportunities to learn new words and expand knowledge of familiar words, building fluency and deepening comprehension	Students read a grade-level complex text in shared reading, including some orthographic mapping, and then practice reading the text independently over time until fluent.

Zooming In on Prioritizing Words for Instruction

Even equipped with a high-frequency word list—whether it is Fry's "Instant Words" (1980) or the 109 most frequently occurring words from Table 4.1—you'll still have some work to do in deciding which words to explicitly teach and when. This might include taking time to reevaluate the order and/or priority of words you teach directly, aligning them to your beginning reading materials and/or your phonics lessons. You will probably want to identify completely decodable words, as well as look for opportunities to group words that have similar spelling patterns. Table 4.5 identifies three types of words to consider as you plan for instruction.

TABLE 4.5

PRIORITIZING HIGH-FREQUENCY WORDS FOR INSTRUCTION

Criteria	Questions for Prioritizing Words	Examples
Irregular + Urgent	Does the word have one or more irregular sound spellings? Does the word appear with high frequency in early texts?	the, of, are, you
Regular + Aligned	Is the word easily decodable? Should it be taught alongside the phonetic concept with which it aligns? Or does it need to be taught sooner?	Short *i*: it, is, in, if CVCe: ate, came, like, made
Irregular + Similar	Is the word spelled with one or more irregular sound spellings? Are there other words that share that same irregularity that could be taught at the same time?	was, want, wash have, love, live could, should, would

Zooming In on Orthographic Mapping

Orthographic mapping is the secret sauce for moving high-frequency words into the visual word form area, eventually converting them to sight words. Let's take a closer look at a specific routine for orthographic mapping. In Table 4.6, we share a guided procedure for aligning the sounds in a word to their spellings. Note how this routine for building lexical quality involves all four processing systems, connecting phonology, orthographics, meaning, and context.

TABLE 4.6

ORTHOGRAPHIC MAPPING ROUTINE

Mapping the Word *Does*	
Say the word and activate meaning.	• "Today we're going to practice an important (funny, interesting, unusual, etc.) word. The word is ***does***." • "Listen while I use ***does*** in a sentence. *My brother does his homework before watching television.*"
Analyze the sounds in the word.	• "Now, close your eyes." • "Listen while I say the word and its sounds slowly." (Say ***does*** slowly; stretching out each continuous phoneme.) • "Say ***does*** slowly to yourself, putting up a finger for each phoneme you hear." • "That's right. It has three sounds." (Repeat and stretch the word. Exaggerate the segmented phoneme by holding out the continuous sounds dŭŭŭzzz.)
Analyze the spelling of the word.	• "Now, watch while I write the letters in ***does*** and say it slowly again." (Write the letters in the word ***does*** as you stretch out the word, saying the phonemes that go with each grapheme as you write them.)

Align sound and spelling.	• "Let me show you the letters that go with each sound in ***does***." (Draw a rectangle around the whole word. Divide the rectangle into individual boxes (Elkonin 1973) around the spellings that represent each phoneme in ***does***.)
	
	    | d | oe | s |
	
	• Move your finger under the word ***does*** as you read it again.
	  • Draw attention to any unfamiliar or irregular spelling patterns. "Isn't that strange? Both the vowel sound and ending sound are surprises! The **/ŭ/** sound is spelled with the letters *oe* and the /z/ sound is spelled with the letter *s*!"

Mapping the Word *Does*	
Practice writing and reading (locking in).	• "Let's read it again." (Let children read it with you as you drag your finger under the word.) • Erase the spelling on your board. • "Now you say *does* slowly, matching each sound as you write it on your board." • "Let's read what you have written." • "Erase *does* and write it one more time."
Connect to meaning and context.	• "Listen while I use *does* to ask a question. *Does* a camel live in the forest? Now, use the word *does* to ask your partner a question. Can you answer your partner's question?"

This process is especially important during the partial and full alphabetic stages, as children are working to develop larger and larger stores of words with high lexical quality. Of course, not every word needs explicit instructional support to become a sight word. Some words are just easier to learn than others. So, be on the lookout for words that seem to call out for more direct practice and be prepared to provide it using the orthographic mapping process in Table 4.6.

Embed high-frequency word learning across the day.

You can easily condense the core elements of mapping speech to print to integrate orthographic mapping throughout the instructional day. In read-aloud, you can pause the reading for a minute, jot an interesting word on the board, and take a few seconds to map the word's sounds onto its spelling. During shared reading, you might pull orthographically interesting words from the text and let students work with partners to align their sounds to their spellings. Guided reading, as well as independent reading and writing conferences, can provide rich opportunities to enhance lexical quality through the orthographic mapping of individual words.

One of our favorite times to take children through a complete orthographic mapping routine is during interactive writing, where they can both watch and practice on their own, using dry erase boards. Writing is important for learning how words work. Give children opportunities to write the words they are learning, saying the sounds (not the letters) as they write the word.

4

Let assessment guide you.

As you work to support beginning readers in developing automaticity with words, you'll want to know *which* words students know. Determining which words are "islands of certainty" (Clay 2015) for students and which are still unknown is especially important when it comes to the list of words in Table 4.1. A checklist of selected high-frequency words can serve as a simple formative assessment tool for keeping track of which individual words students can read and write.

As you assess high-frequency words, you will want to determine which words have become truly automatic—that is, which words children can read or write fluently—not just which words students can figure out.

Although we do advocate assessing sight word knowledge specifically, we suggest that this is most important for the first 100 words or so. We do not recommend testing children with hundreds of flash cards across the primary grades. Once children know simple steps for mapping speech to print, have working knowledge of the alphabetic system, and begin collecting orthographic knowledge through self-teaching (Share 1995, 1999, 2004), isolated teaching and testing of high-frequency words become less important (Solity and Vousden 2009).

▼ ▼ ▼ ▲ ▼ ▼

Meanwhile, Back in the Classroom . . .

After recently learning about orthographic mapping, Ms. Ellis has been rethinking the routines she uses for teaching high-frequency words to her first-grade students. To get started, she has decided to become more systematic about the way she teaches children the most common irregularly spelled words. She sees several opportunities to embed this practice into her regular reading and writing work with students.

She begins by studying the children's writing to identify frequently misspelled words. She finds the words *they* and *want* are often misspelled by many students, and she decides to intentionally teach them during interactive writing.

She includes the whole class in composing a thank-you note to Kara, who recently gave them a tour on their field trip to the zoo. Ms. Ellis assembles the children on the floor with dry erase boards and markers. After engaging them in a conversation about their trip and collecting the children's ideas, she works with them to decide on three sentences to follow the greeting "Dear Kara":

> *We liked the baby animals. They were so cute. We want to*
> *come back.*

Ms. Ellis alternates between letting the children write some words and writing the words herself. Although she doesn't take time to map every word, Ms. Ellis takes particular care with the word *they*. She asks the children to close their eyes and listen as she says the word *they* slowly, so they can count the sounds they hear in the word. When the children open their eyes, she has them listen to *they* again as she holds up a finger for each of the two sounds.

Then, Ms. Ellis writes the word *they* on the white board, saying the two sounds "/th/-/ā/" as she writes the letters. Next, she draws a rectangle around the whole word and asks the children to notice which letters go with which sounds. She draws a line between the *th* and the *ey*, creating Elkonin boxes (Elkonin 1973) around each part of the word, saying /th/ and / ā /, and pointing to indicate which letters go with which sounds.

Ms. Ellis says, "Isn't that funny?! There isn't even an *A* in *they*! In *they*, the /ā/ sound is made by *ey*!" She models pointing to the letters as she says the sounds in *they* once more.

The children write *they* on their dry erase boards and blend through the word a couple of times, pointing to the letters that go with each of the two sounds as they are pronounced.

Finally, the children chorally read everything written in the letter so far and continue adding to their thank-you note. The whole mapping process takes about two minutes, and Ms. Ellis repeats it when they get to the word *want*.

A few days later, during whole-group word study time, Ms. Ellis asks all the children to write a dictation sentence that combines the focus sight words (*they*, *want*) with her current phonics focus (long vowels spelled with a final *e*). She dictates the sentence "They want a bite of cake." When she collects their papers, she finds that all but two students spelled both *they* and *want* correctly. Ms. Ellis plans to give extra practice to these two students and to select a text for small-group reading that will provide additional encounters with the new words.

Questions for Reflection

Checking In with Yourself: What were you previously taught about high-frequency word instruction? How is the learning in this shift similar to (or different from) that?

High-Frequency Word Selection: How will you choose which high-frequency words to teach, and in what order?

Decodable Words: How might you go about identifying high-frequency words that are completely regular (decodable) and embedding them into your aligned phonics instruction?

Grouping: How will you group words with similar features, patterns, or meanings so that your instruction is efficient and the words are easier for students to learn?

Orthographic Mapping: How will you establish orthographic mapping routines to strengthen lexical quality and lock words into memory? How might you make orthographic mapping a part of your instructional contexts (shared reading, interactive writing, small-group instruction, etc.)?

Differentiation: Who do your current practices for word learning best serve? Who will benefit the most from a shift in practice?

Assessment: How are you currently collecting data about student knowledge of irregularly spelled high-frequency words? How do you use this information to inform your instructional choices? What next steps might you consider?

Reinventing the Ways We Use MSV (3 Cueing Systems)

Ms. Sanchez, a second-grade teacher, is at the guided reading table listening in and coaching as her students read today's text, *What Do Birds Eat?* An anchor chart behind her shows a cumulative list of strategies she has taught across time.

Ms. Sanchez uses running records as well as anecdotal notes to record what readers do in the moment as they navigate text during small-group instruction. Running records help her identify instructional goals for each reader as she reflects on each child's use of the strategies she has already taught.

SHIFT

Stuck on a word?
Try a Strategy!

 Look at the picture for clues.

 Skip the word and go on.

 Look for parts you know.

 Flip the sound.

 Try a word that makes sense.

Jonah is prone to freezing up and waiting for help from the teacher when he comes to unknown words. Ms. Sanchez's goal for him is to get him to more consistently "try something" at the point of difficulty, rather than stopping or waiting for help. But today, after watching him stop and stare at the page blankly for several minutes, Ms. Sanchez joins Jonah to offer a nudge.

"Jonah, have you run into something tricky?" she asks. Jonah points to the word *favorite* in the sentence "Seeds and nuts are a *favorite* snack for many birds." "I can't figure out this word," he says. "I already tried looking for parts I know. I see *it* and *or*, but I still can't think of any words that make sense there. I don't know what else to try." Ms. Sanchez reflects on the strategy list herself. She realizes that Jonah has, in fact, tried two of the strategies she's taught but is still stuck and still frustrated.

After coaching Jonah, Ms. Sanchez moves on to Mateo. Lately, she has been encouraging Mateo to think about what would make sense when he gets to a tricky word. Today, she is pleased to see that when he encounters the word *branches*, he doesn't hesitate before skipping the word and moving on: "Hidden up in the _____ of a tree, the baby birds . . ." He doesn't even have to read to the end of the sentence before he knows what the word is. "*Branches*! It's *branches*!"

Ms. Sanchez wants him to check his prediction, so she asks, "Does that make sense?" Mateo nods confidently and resumes reading, without taking time to even look at the word or reread to double-check it. He *is* right, of course. The word is *branches*. But as she shifts her attention to Chloe, Ms. Sanchez finds herself wondering if getting the word "right," without really even looking at the word, is enough.

Chloe's reading has left Ms. Sanchez more and more puzzled lately. Chloe is agentive and quick to try multiple strategies at the point of difficulty. She has rich vocabulary and deep background knowledge. So when she comes to tricky words, Chloe doesn't stall out like Jonah, but instead considers the first few sounds and, with relative ease, generates a word choice that makes some sense in the context of the sentence.

Her running records seem to imply that Chloe is consistently using a balance of meaning, structure, and visual (MSV) information to solve problems. Still, Ms. Sanchez has a nagging concern about a decline in Chloe's overall accuracy and is also confused that, even though Chloe always opts to use meaning first at the point of difficulty, her comprehension seems to be on the decline.

Ms. Sanchez is working hard to give her students a wide range of strategies for their problem-solving toolboxes, and they are working hard to apply these strategies in text at the point of difficulty. But despite an anchor chart full of strategies, her students still seem to encounter many unproductive detours and dead ends as they navigate their texts. Understandably, Ms. Sanchez is concerned.

A COMMON PRACTICE TO RECONSIDER

▼ ▼ ▼ ▼ ▲ ▼

Treating decoding as a strategy of last resort.

Perhaps you have experienced something similar to Ms. Sanchez, recognizing that your best efforts to know your students as readers haven't translated into the success you want for them.

Much of the strategy work Ms. Sanchez has offered her students—teaching them to skip the word, to rely heavily on context, and to think of something that makes sense—originates in a model of reading instruction familiar to many of us. This model, generally referred to as MSV, or the three cueing systems, is presented in Figure 5.1. Because MSV was originally shared primarily through workshops rather than books, it is hard to trace its true origins (Adams 1998). Still, many of us have been taught to use this model to respond to children as they work through unknown words, or tricky spots, in text.

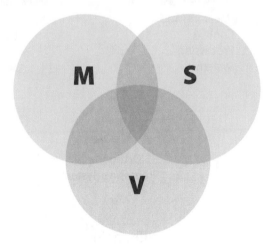

Figure 5.1 Meaning, Structure, Visual (MSV)

5

In the MSV model, *M* represents *meaning*, or the contextual supports a reader can draw on when trying to figure out an unknown word. Meaning includes background knowledge, picture clues, vocabulary, familiarity with story structure, and so on. To prompt a student to attend to meaning cues, a teacher might say, "What would make sense?" or "Did that make sense?" (Pinnell 2008; Pinnell and Fountas 2009; Clay 2013, 2015, 2017; Fountas and Pinnell 2016). Meaning in the MSV model includes the work of both the meaning and context processing systems from the Four-Part Processing Model, which we described in Shift 1.

The *S* in the MSV model represents *structure*, or the syntactical information in the text that can help a reader figure out an unknown word. Structure includes drawing on what you know about grammar or word order. To prompt toward structure, a teacher might say, "What would sound right?" or "Did that sound right?" (Pinnell 2008; Pinnell and Fountas 2009; Clay 2013, 2015, 2017; Fountas and Pinnell 2016). Structure in the MSV model involves both the meaning processing system—because our meaning of a word can include knowledge of the way it functions—and the context processing systems from the Four-Part Processing Model.

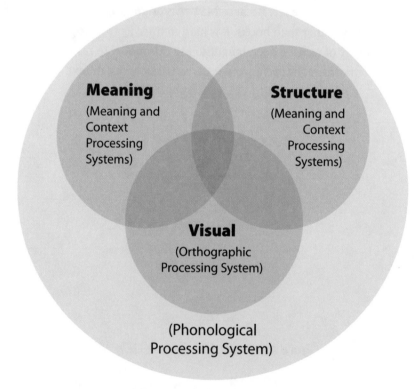

Figure 5.2 Connecting MSV and the Four-Part Processing Model

Finally, the *V* represents *visual*, or letters and letter patterns (orthographic information) available to help a reader figure out an unknown word. To prompt students to look at the visual information, a teacher might say, "Get your mouth ready" or "Does that look right?" (Pinnell 2008; Pinnell and Fountas 2009; Clay 2013, 2015, 2017; Fountas and Pinnell 2016). Visual information in the MSV model includes the work of the orthographic processing system.

The relationship between the systems in the Four-Part Processing Model and the MSV model is illustrated in Figure 5.2. You will notice that the work of the phonological processing system is not explicitly represented by the MSV model, although it is intrinsic to all three of its parts (Adams 1990; Seidenberg and McClelland 1989; Seidenberg 2017).

In addition to guiding the work we do with readers as they problem solve, the three sources of information (M, S, V) are also used to analyze reading behaviors at the point of difficulty. By doing a running record and miscue analysis, we can think about which sources of information children use or neglect when they encounter a tricky word. The goal, as many balanced literacy teachers have come to understand it, is to look for evidence that students are using a "balance" of meaning, structure, and visual information and, if not, to specifically coach into any neglected sources of information. Table 5.1 compares the ways the model is typically used both to prompt children during reading and to analyze reading behaviors after.

TABLE 5.1

TRADITIONAL USE OF MSV DURING AND AFTER READING

Source of Information	Prompting DURING Reading	Analyzing Reading Behavior AFTER Reading
Traditional use of Meaning	**Word Solving:** "What would make sense?" **Checking:** "Does that make sense?"	Did the miscue make sense in context? **Example** (Miscue on the word *horse*): "It is feeding time for the **pony**." (**Makes sense**) "It is feeding time for the **house**." (**Does not make sense**)

continues

Source of Information	Prompting DURING Reading	Analyzing Reading Behavior AFTER Reading
Traditional use of Structure	**Word Solving:** "What would sound right?" **Checking:** "Does that sound right?"	Does the miscue sound right grammatically? **Example** (Miscue on the word *went*): "I **want** to the store." **(Does not sound right)** "I **walked** to the store." **(Sounds right)**
Traditional use of Visual	**Word Solving:** "Get your mouth ready." **Checking:** "Does it match?"	Did some part of the miscue match the letters of the actual word? **Example** (Miscue on the word *hammer*): "The **handle** is on the table." **(Matches)** "The **tool** is on the table." **(Does not match)**

Adapted from Pinnell and Fountas (2009), Pinnell (2008)

Generally speaking, the three-circle Venn diagram, as a representation of three sources of information for readers, makes scientific sense (Adams 1998). It is true that proficient readers use a text's meaning, structure, and visual information to read. But the work our brains do with each of these sources of information is a bit different than most of us were taught, and the equal importance of each source of information—inherent in the MSV model's three equal circles—is often lost in its interpretation (Adams 1998; Seidenberg 2017).

Clearing Up Some Confusion

Even if this three-circle Venn diagram is new to you, if you are a balanced literacy practitioner, it is likely that your work is influenced by it. Although the MSV model has helped many teachers think deeply about children's reading processes, some not-so-helpful trickle-down effects of this model—from strategy instruction that teaches children to skip over words to Beanie Baby visuals as reminders for strategy use—are widespread.

If MSV is *not* new to you, chances are this model is deeply rooted in your foundational beliefs about how children read. That might make a conversation about its limitations—such as the one we offer in the upcoming sections— a bit scary. It certainly did for us.

MISUNDERSTANDING:

We need to avoid telling students to "sound it out."

Many of us were taught (and in turn taught others) to avoid the dreaded words *sound it out*. This prompt has received so much criticism that, for many of us, its use invites self-doubt, and even shame. In fact, Kari's heart beats a bit faster at the very idea.

A learned reluctance to say "sound it out" can leave us trying to teach for balance without adequate use of one of the three potential sources of information. Minimizing use of visual information actually makes learning to read harder. But learning to read is hard enough already. We certainly wouldn't knowingly do anything that would make the process more difficult for children. Yet, this minimization of visual information—whether intentional or not—results in instruction that looks more like the imbalance shown in Figure 5.3 than the evenly weighted Figure 5.1.

So, the idea that prompting children to study the print is an instructional move to minimize is misguided at best and can actually make learning to

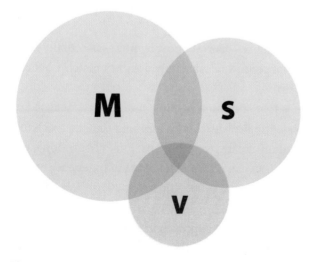

Figure 5.3 The Reality of Common MSV Implementations

5

read a whole lot harder for many children, in the long run (Perfetti 1985; Seidenberg 2017).

It is true, however, that simply saying "sound it out" is insufficient for teaching children to read. So, as we reclaim this prompt to visual information, children will also need explicit instruction, modeling, and practice to learn what the "sound it out" call to action really means.

Still, all of this talk about visual information may leave you wondering, "But isn't meaning most important? Shouldn't children use multiple sources of information? And can't they do a lot of inferring without studying every little bit of print?" These are all really great questions that we will tackle in the following sections, as we explore what the science tells us and some of the reasons using visual information seems to have gotten a really bad rap.

MISUNDERSTANDING:

When they are problem solving, children should first ask, "What would make sense?"

We don't think anyone—whether a proponent of "the science of reading" or balanced literacy, or both—will argue that reading is *all* about meaning making. To read without meaning is simply to say words.

So, if there are three sources of information available for readers—meaning, structure, visual—prioritizing meaning while problem solving just makes good sense.

Or does it?

Sometimes science—as you know by now—is actually counterintuitive. And sometimes what seems logical simply does not match what really goes on inside a reader's brain.

The issue is that, although helping children stay focused on comprehension seems completely logical, teaching a meaning-first approach to figuring out tricky words can actually create two problems. First, it cuts down on the orthographic knowledge children can accumulate, making independent reading less valuable in the long run (Adams 1990; Kilpatrick 2016). We offer more about this in Misunderstanding 4.

Second, a meaning-first approach to individual word solving teaches children an unsustainable process for figuring out words. This is because contextual support for individual words actually decreases as the complexity and concept density in texts increases (Kamhi and Catts 2012; Gough, Alford, and Holley-Wilcox 1981; Gough and Wren 1998). So, teaching children to rely first and foremost on context for figuring out words is teaching them a process that will eventually fall apart on them.

If that's not reason enough to revisit "sound it out," there's more.

Focusing on meaning first, instead of the visual information (orthography), when figuring out words can compromise the important role that meaning and structure really *do* play in problem solving words. Meaning and structure actually work together to do two word-solving jobs for readers. That is, once the reader has made an attempt at the word by using the print, *then* meaning and context swoop in, drawing on language comprehension to either make the leap to the correct word (set for variability) or to cross-check the accuracy of the word.

So, rather than teaching print as the strategy of last resort, you can teach it as the strategy of first resort, showing children at every stage of development how to look closely at words, and setting them up for sense-making success. This will probably involve revising the general way you interpret the MSV Venn diagram, broadening your definitions of M, S, and V (refer to Figure 5.2), and changing from an implementation that looks like this:

M s v

to an interpretation of the model that assigns as much value to print as it does to meaning and structure (think the Simple View of Reading!), like this:

V→MS

By teaching children to *start* with print and to *follow* their print attempts with checking any or all of the three cueing systems, you reinvent the MSV model, making it V→MS, and better aligning it with science, including the Simple View of Reading. Figure 5.4 shows the ways V→MS aligns with the Simple View of Reading (SVR).

5

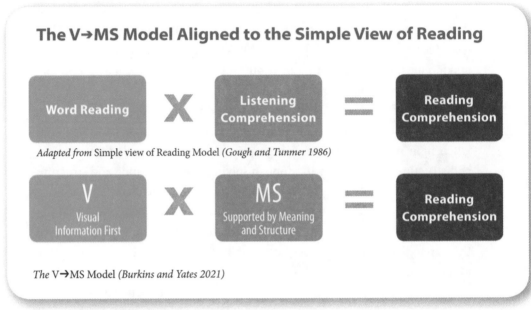

Figure 5.4 The V→MS Model Aligned to the Simple View of Reading

Those of us who have relied on MSV for a long time have an opportunity to make relatively simple but critical adjustments to a model we hold dear. By reorganizing our prompting priorities to elevate the use of visual information, we situate meaning and structure to better support making the leap to the correct word, cross-checking for accuracy, and sense-making. This change aligns the whole model with science and actually better equips students to construct meaning from text.

MISUNDERSTANDING:

Children don't need to use all of the print to read.

Although theories about readers "sampling letters" across words are popular and strategies for letter sampling are often taught to young readers, eye movement technology makes the experimental science on this topic clear. Proficient readers do not sample some letters and skip others (Dehaene 2009; Willingham 2017; Seidenberg 2017).

Maybe you have even participated in an exercise where many letters have been omitted from words and yet you're still able to "read" the sentence with relatively little struggle. Here, try this example. Can you figure it out?

T•m••••w •s m• b•••d•y. I •••'t w••t!

With a little effort, and seemingly very few print clues, you probably figured it out—*Tomorrow is my birthday. I can't wait!* An exercise such as this one might lead you to believe that you can read without attending to all the letters in a word.

However, this example actually illustrates the opposite.

The truth is, you would not have been able to figure out the word *tomorrow*, for example, if you didn't already have a high-quality lexical representation (Perfetti and Hart 2002; Perfetti 2007) of the word filed away of the word form area of your brain! So the sentence with all the missing letters actually illustrates the *importance* of accumulating a whole lot of orthographic (visual) information that you can retrieve when you need it. Where did this orthographic knowledge come from? It came from looking closely at all the visual information in lots and lots of words (Dehaene 2009; Willingham 2017; Seidenberg 2017), in other words, lots of reading!

Because children are learning a complex alphabetic system, any efforts to minimize close scrutiny of the print—such as looking at only a few letters and letting context or structure do the rest—eliminates a chance to really learn the word. The trade-off for skipping deep orthographic work in the short run is less orthographic knowledge—and less fluency *and less comprehension*—in the long run.

Remember Chloe from the beginning of the chapter? She is a prime example of a student relying on bits and pieces of print, but not on *nearly enough* visual information. She flew through emergent-level, predictable readers. But as texts have gotten longer and filled with an increasing number of multisyllabic words—relying on a few letters and context has long since ceased to be effective.

So, although it is true that the readers in Ehri's partial alphabetic phase tend to sample prominent letters and consider the context (often a picture cue) to figure out the word, this tendency should be treated as a temporary, albeit normal, phase of reading development (Ehri 2002; Moats and Tolman 2019). And even students who are developmentally in this first-letter-and-what-makes-sense phase need to be taught to look closely at all the visual information in a word as they are trying to figure it out. In other words, we have to help children get *to* the meaning by going *through* the words rather than *around* them (Dehaene 2009; Kilpatrick 2016; Willingham 2017; Seidenberg 2017).

4 MISUNDERSTANDING:

The primary reason to teach children to decode is to problem solve the word in the moment.

When readers are stuck on a word, can feel as if the main goal is to help them get *that* word, so they can get back to sense-making. If children are stymied, frustration is building, and fluency is halting, helping readers move past the tricky word in front of them can feel like the priority, in the moment.

But actually, doing the work of decoding offers much more than an immediate remedy.

It turns out the real value of decoding a word *is not* in figuring out *the* word! The underappreciated yet critical value in any encounter with an unknown word, especially for beginning readers, is how it adds to children's learned store of letter sequences (orthographic knowledge), preparing them to read *future* words fluently (Kilpatrick 2016; Seidenberg 2017).

Figure 5.5 illustrates the long-term value of encouraging beginning readers to make use of the print. It shows the long-term value of decoding.

As Figure 5.5 illustrates, decoding is just the tip of the learning-to-read iceberg. Decoding words is only the beginning of the work of accumulating orthographic knowledge in a systematic way. Early and frequent decoding experiences facilitate orthographic mapping, which increases orthographic learning. This domino effect helps readers send more words to long-term storage in the visual word form area, where they can be retrieved fluently and automatically, freeing up more and more attention for comprehension. So, each encounter with decoding and orthographic mapping positions children to establish what Clay refers to as a "self-extending system" (Clay 1993, 17).

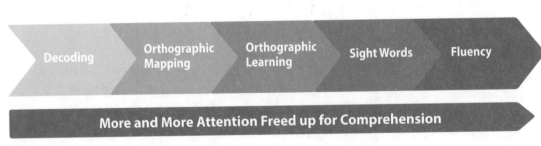

Figure 5.5 The Path from Decoding to Fluency

A Short Summary of the Science

▲ MSV is a common reading model used in many balanced literacy classrooms.

▲ In aligning the MSV model with the Four-Part Processing Model, *Visual* represents the orthographic processing system. *Meaning* and *Structure* represent both meaning and context processing systems.

▲ Phonological processing is not explicitly represented in MSV but is implicit to all three cueing systems.

▲ Meaning (including illustrations) *and* language structure are important sources of information for making the leap from an approximation to the actual word (set for variability) and for cross-checking word-solving attempts.

▲ Building automaticity with word recognition is essential for fluency and comprehension because it frees up attention for sense-making.

▲ Each experience with a word strengthens neural pathways within and between the four processing systems. These connections deepen lexical quality, supporting the automatic word recognition that frees attention for comprehension.

▲ Teaching children to rely on context as the strategy of first resort can keep them locked in earlier phases of reading development.

▲ Proficient readers attend to every bit of visual information, looking sequentially from left to right. They do not skip or sample letters.

▲ As texts get more difficult, context becomes less and less helpful for figuring out individual words.

▲ The beginning reader's slow decoding work leads to the long-term benefits of orthographic mapping, eventual fluency, and better comprehension.

5

THE SIMPLE AND SCIENTIFICALLY SOUND SHIFT

▼ ▼ ▼ ▼ ▲ ▼

Prioritize print as a strategy of first resort for word solving, using meaning and structure to cross-check.

Recommendations for Making the Shift

This shift has given you the chance to look courageously at some ideas that have been foundational in the balanced literacy classroom. To help you make the science in this shift actionable as you sit next to readers, we offer the following instructional recommendations.

Learn to use a few high-leverage instructional routines to support problem solving.

In the Table 5.2, we describe a few instructional routines worth considering to help students make the most of all three sources of information—visual, meaning, and structure—considering how they overlap with the Four-Part Processing Model. We zoom in on three of these routines in the sections that follow: starting with visual, rereading, and taking a tricky word to writing.

TABLE 5.2

HIGH-LEVERAGE INSTRUCTIONAL ROUTINES TO SUPPORT PROBLEM SOLVING WORDS

The What: *Routine*	The Why: *Purpose*	The How: *Examples*
Practice patience.	To give students time to problem solve before jumping in (Burkins and Yaris 2016), and to avoid creating dependency on you rather than on the text and on themselves	When a student hesitates on a word, give them enough time to think and problem solve on their own. Watch and make note of what you observe as you wait.
Touch the text.	To offer a nonverbal reminder that the most powerful support for them lies in learning to study the text	When a student stops reading and looks at you, touching or simply looking at the text can serve as a gentle nudge toward the print, reminding the student that it contains helpful information.
Look before you leap.	To support building long-term orthographic knowledge and sustainable problem-solving strategies	When a child is stuck on a tricky word, encourage them to start by looking carefully at the word, rather than first directing them to go to the pictures or other contextual support.

continues

The What: *Routine*	The Why: *Purpose*	The How: *Examples*
Make the leap.	To teach children to use context and structure to make a leap from their phonetic approximation to a word they know (set for variability).	When a child sounds through a word and comes up with an approximation that is close but not quite right (e.g., **/kŏwə/ instead of cow**), you can nudge students to access their phonological lexicon: "Do you know a word that sounds a bit like /kŏwə/ and makes sense here?"
Reread to cross-check.	To teach children to reread, using their meaning and context processing systems (meaning and structure), to confirm the phonetic attempt	After a child uses visual information to problem solve a word, you can say, "Reread. Does that make sense?"
Take a closer look.	To lift the tricky word out of the text, enlarging it in writing for closer visual inspection and orthographic mapping	When a child is stuck on the word *together*, you write the word on a whiteboard looking carefully at the orthography of the word.

Zooming In on Look Before You Leap

As you know by now, the problem-solving route for sense-making can reliably begin with visual information, so that meaning and structure (the meaning and context processing systems) are positioned to do their jobs well. Figure 5.6 illustrates the V→MS path to sense-making when problem solving a tricky word.

Until students have learned the Look Before You Leap process in Figure 5.6, each step along the path requires thoughtful instructional language. In Figure 5.7, we offer some specific language examples you can use with children to help them practice the V→MS path. You can also download a copy at **TheSixShifts.com**.

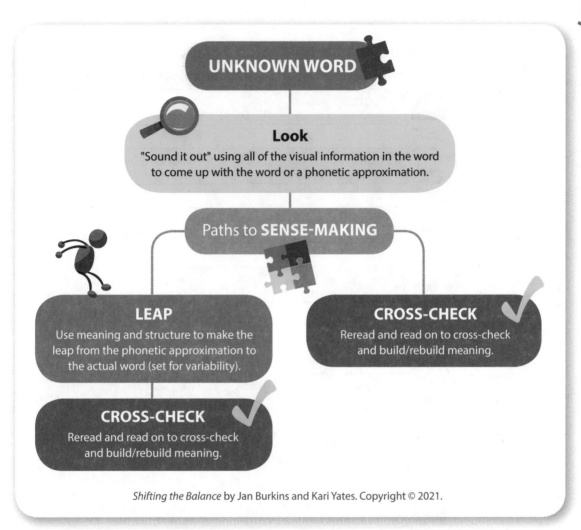

Figure 5.6 The Look Before You Leap Routine: Paths to Problem Solving Using V→MS

A bonus of the visual information first approach is that readers learn a consistent process—*first* carefully study the print from left to right, *then* check using meaning and structure—rather than sorting through a long list of possible strategies on the run and applying them in a hit-or-miss fashion. Of course, you certainly wouldn't use all of the supports in Figure 5.7 in a single interaction with a child. Also, expect readers to take recursive action while problem solving—starting with print, checking the meaning, going back to the print, and so on.

Look: Start with the Print

	To Get Students To:	You Might Say Something Like:
	DECODE before using other strategies.	"Start with the letters." "Look at the letters first."
	LOOK carefully at each part of the word.	"Make every sound." "Look at every letter."
	STAY focused on the print.	"Keep your eyes on the letters." "Stick with it until the end."
	BLEND all the sounds together.	"Put the sounds together." "Smooth it out."

Leap: Add Context

	To Get Students To:	You Might Say Something Like:
	LEAP from the phonetic approximation to the word.	"What word does that sound like?"
	CHECK the word to move on or problem-solve more.	"Does that make sense?" "Does that sound right?"
	REBUILD meaning after problem-solving.	"Reread the sentence."

Shifting the Balance by Jan Burkins and Kari Yates. Copyright © 2021.

Figure 5.7 Utilizing Visual Information for Sense-making

Zooming In on Rereading

Explicitly teaching students to reread, rather than rushing off down the page after they think they've solved a tricky word, is critical. Rereading helps readers:

▲ Make the leap from the almost right word to the actual word.

▲ Confirm (or eliminate) word choices during/after problem solving.

▲ Compare the word's orthography with its phonological structure.

▲ Rebuild meaning after interrupting fluency to engage in problem solving.

▲ Get a second look at a tricky word (and all the words around it), therefore, increasing its lexical quality (Perfetti and Hart 2002; Perfetti 2007) and contributing to future automaticity.

Rereading is really "listening again" during reading. So, when readers are encouraged to reread, thinking about whether their attempt makes sense or sounds right, they are tapping into their listening comprehension to check on the decoding. Rereading brings all four parts of the Four-Part Processing System together for one final check of the spoken language that has been unlocked from the print.

Zooming In on Taking Tricky Words to Writing for Closer Analysis

Sometimes while reading with a child, you might decide to grab a sheet of paper or whiteboard and "lift" a particular word out of the text for a closer look. This decision to "take a word to writing" is a powerful way to guide a student in looking carefully (analytically) at all of the letters in the word from left to right (visual/orthographic information), working out how the sounds (phonology) and the letters align (Clay 1993, 2016). If this seems familiar, it's because taking words to writing involves guided decoding, followed by orthographic mapping, which we explored in Shift 4.

Here we share a step-by-step process for lifting a word out of text, analyzing it, and taking it back to the book; Figure 5.8 shows an example.

1. Lift the word out of the text, working from print to speech first (decoding).

    a. Write the word, breaking it into chunks (fla·min·go).

    b. Guide the student in blending the sounds in the word, chunk by chunk to make an approximation.

    c. Provide support in "making the leap" from approximation to a known word (*flamingo*).

    d. Offer a definition, if the word is new to the child. ("It's a long-legged pink bird.")

2. Now that the word is known, move from speech back to print (orthographic mapping).

    a. Say the word slowly, moving your finger under each part. Have the student repeat the process.
    b. Erase the word and write it one more time, or have the student write it.

3. Take the word "back to the book." Let the student cover the word with a finger and reveal the chunks bit by bit.

4. Have the student reread the word in the context of the sentence ("But a flamingo loves to eat shrimp").

Of course it wouldn't be efficient to use this strategy with every tricky word. The words that are most powerful to analyze in this way are words with features that students have already been studying, that they will be learning soon, or that are especially high leverage. For instance, the example in Figure 5.8 has an initial consonant blend, two syllables with simple short vowel patterns, and

Shifting the Balance by Jan Burkins and Kari Yates. Copyright © 2021.

Figure 5.8 Taking a Word to Writing for Closer Analysis

the known word chunk *go*, so studying those letter strings can give students valuable orthographic building blocks they can use to read new words.

Let assessment guide you.

When completing an error analysis in a running record, many teachers have been taught to "give students credit" if they use any visual information at all, as long as there is a discernible match between the miscue and the actual word. For instance, "*pat*" for *point*, "kite" for *kitten*, and "dictation" for *different* are typically considered indications that the student is attending to the visual characteristics of the word.

When analyzing a reader's miscues, however, you can avoid all-or-none thinking, especially regarding the use of visual information. By analyzing which parts of the miscues match the words on the page—noting alignment at the beginning, middle, and the end of the word—you can find telling patterns in students' reading behaviors. Figure 5.9 shows an example of a simple modification to a standard running record form, with space for more elaboration on the depth of visual information used.

For example, when a child says "candle" for *camper*, we might traditionally indicate on a running record that the child *is* using visual information, because the first part of the miscue aligns with the word. However, if we look at the

Sample V→MS Miscue Analysis

Student: Text: *What Birds Eat*		Decoding			Sense- Making		Self- Correcting
What the student said	**What the text said**	V_B	V_M	V_E	M	S	SC
high	*hidden*	✓	—	—	✓	✓	—
break	*branches*	✓	—	—	?	✓	—
watching	*waiting*	✓	—	✓	✓	✓	—

Figure 5.9 Sample V→MS Miscue Analysis

beginning, middle, and end of the attempt (V_B V_M V_E) and look for patterns across miscues, we can learn much more about how well students are using visual information *across entire words*. For example, the student in this sample is overlooking much of the visual information and counting on meaning and structure to fill in the blanks. We need to ask, "*How well* are students using visual information?" rather than simply asking whether they are using visual information or not.

For more elaboration on revising the ways you use running records, see *Preventing Misguided Reading* (Burkins and Croft 2017). To download a PDF of the V→MS Miscue Analysis Form, go to **TheSixShifts.com**/downloadables.

Meanwhile, Back in the Classroom . . .

Ms. Sanchez has recently joined a professional inquiry circle focused on fluency strategies for beginning readers. The group has read several journal articles, listened to a series of podcasts, and explored some websites and white papers. The learning and conversation have been thought provoking and challenging but Ms. Sanchez finds herself looking forward to these discussions with her colleagues each Wednesday afternoon.

As a result of her learning, she's made some adjustments to the practices that drive her small-group instruction.

One idea that has surprised her from the beginning was hearing from a variety of sources that "sound it out" didn't have to be avoided after all. This news has felt like a giant relief to Ms. Sanchez. To her, it had always made sense to simply have students start with the letters in front of them when solving tricky words, but she'd been frequently coached to steer children away from decoding and toward relying first on the meaning.

She's also been pondering the separate but related idea that instead of a whole bunch of novel strategies for word solving, kids might only need a few really ordinary and dependable ones—starting with the print, rereading, making the leap, and cross-checking.

Because she realizes that a change in her own thinking will translate into a different approach for her readers as well, she decides that shared reading is the most efficient context for introducing this shift. She starts the lesson by saying, "Readers, does this ever happen to you? You come to a tricky word and you're wondering what to do. You look at the strategy chart, and you feel like there are so many different ideas or things to try that you have a hard time choosing."

Jonah nods his head vigorously. "It happens to me all the time," he says without hesitation.

"Well, beginning today, let's decide to always start with the same strategy. Today, when we come to a tricky word, let's look closely at the letters and words *first*, and see what we can figure out. Then, we can reread to be sure our reading makes sense and sounds right. Watch, as I show you what this looks like."

Ms. Sanchez demonstrates the process of problem solving the word *waffle* in the sentence "I had a waffle for breakfast," which she had written on the board. Next, in the big book they are reading together, she finds a few additional strategic opportunities to engage children in the shared work of using visual information as the strategy of first resort, making the leap when necessary, and finally rereading to cross-check. Following shared reading, Ms. Sanchez is eager to see who will apply this revised thinking on their own.

During small-group instruction, as the children gather to read *Caring for a New Puppy*, Ms. Sanchez turns her attention first to Jonah, who gets stuck on the first page. When she asks, "How's it going?" Jonah shakes his head and points to the word *company*. "I can't get this word. I looked at all the letters like you said, but it's still really hard." Ms. Sanchez says, "Let's look at it together. Watch while I write it." Ms. Sanchez writes *com pan y* on a page of her notebook and says, "Run your finger under each part." Surprisingly, as soon as Jonah sees the word enlarged and in chunks, he easily figures out the word. Once he has decoded *company*, Ms. Sanchez gets Jonah to stretch the word back out, rereading as he runs his finger under the word to compare the sounds he's saying to the print. Next, she has him find the word in his text again and use his finger to reveal it chunk by chunk. Finally, he rereads the sentence to pick up steam, have one more exposure to the word, and rebuild meaning.

Mateo is next. He is working on the sentence, "Different breeds of puppies need different things to be healthy and happy." He reads most of the sentence, hesitates momentarily, and then quickly skips over the word *healthy*. When he gets to the end of the sentence, Ms. Sanchez says, "Rather than skip the word, try looking closely." Mateo goes back to the first word and reads again, "Different breeds of puppies need different things to be *heethy* and happy." "Read it again." He repeats the sentence with his attempt—"Different breeds of dogs need different things to be *heethy* and happy," and then pauses to think. "Aah, it's healthy!" he announces as he "makes the leap." Ms. Sanchez says, "Look carefully one more time and see if that matches." As Mateo does this slow reread of the word, aligning letters and sounds for *healthy*, he is orthographically mapping a word with an unexpected vowel sound spelling.

Chloe is reading the sentence "Puppies need a lot of exercise." She slows down at the word *exercise*, making the first two sounds "ex" and then shifting her gaze, away from the print deep in thought. She even repeats the sentence to herself, "Puppies need a lot of ex . . . ex . . . extras. Puppies need a lot of extras." She nods her head confidently and continues on to the next sentence.

Ms. Sanchez stops her. "Did that make sense, Chloe?" Chloe nods, "Yes. Like puppies need lots of extra things." Ms. Sanchez sees the familiar pattern. Chloe is using meaning and initial visual information but not looking carefully across the whole word. Even when the word choice doesn't really fit, Chloe uses her strong background knowledge to *make it* make sense to her!

Ms. Sanchez says, "Look closely at that word, running your finger under all the letters as you slowly say the sounds in *extra*." Chloe stretches out the sounds in *extra* as she drags her finger under the word. "It doesn't match," she says.

"So, try it again, and read across the whole word chunk by chunk. "Ex—er—kiss. . . exerkiss . . . exerkize . . . ex-er-cise. *Exercise*. It's exercise!" She says, eyes lighting. "Now read the whole sentence to check it." Chloe rereads, "Puppies need lots of exercise." Chloe grins, "Oh, that does make more sense." As they finish their work together, Ms. Sanchez reminds her, "Anytime you come to a tricky word, you can read across the whole word chunk by chunk, and then reread to see if it makes sense."

Questions for Reflection

Checking In with Yourself: What is your experience with MSV, and how does the information in this shift align with or disrupt it? Has your thinking changed? If so, how?

Patience: How will you ensure that students have ample processing time before you offer prompts or other supports?

Prioritizing Print: What steps do you need to take to intentionally and consistently teach students to prioritize (rather than minimize) visual information when problem solving unknown words?

Set for Variability: How will you teach children to listen to their own phonemic approximations, search their phonological lexicons for similar words, and "make the leap" to the known word?

Rereading: In your current practice, when do you notice yourself prompting students to reread? How can you support students in developing habits for systematically rereading at the word and/or sentence level, leveraging oral language for sense-making?

Assessment: What formative data are you currently collecting to better understand student miscues and problem solving at the point of difficulty? What next steps might you consider?

Reconsidering Texts for Beginning Readers

I t's time for the literacy block in Ms. Quinn's kindergarten classroom. Ms. Quinn is deeply committed to readers spending time with eyes on print, as well as having opportunities to develop oral language using beloved trade literature. Therefore, all of her students have many self-selected trade books for independent reading, and they know how to read these books in a variety of ways: reading the pictures, retelling a familiar story using "book language," and sometimes even reading the words. Each day, everyone spends some time with their self-selected texts while Ms. Quinn works with small groups.

At the small-group table, students begin each session by warming up with familiar texts from previous lessons. Today Farhia begins with a text called *At the Store*. The book lists many different foods that a young girl likes at the grocery store. Farhia reads slowly and carefully, pointing to each word and referring to the pictures for help with the pattern changes. "I like . . . apples. I like . . . bananas." Ms. Quinn reinforces Farhia's cross-checking: "You're checking the picture and looking at the words. That's an important way to help yourself as a reader."

On the page that shows a picture of a box of cereal, Farhia reads, "I like . . . /k/ . . . /k/ . . . crackers." Pleased with her success she says, "It starts like *cat*." Ms. Quinn nods. The box indeed could be a box of crackers, were it not for the bowl and the milk. "Look more closely at the picture," Ms. Quinn says. "What else could it be?" Farhia tries again, saying, "/k/ . . . /k/ . . ." but eventually shrugs her shoulders and says, "I don't know. It looks like *cereal*, but *cereal* starts with /s/ like *snake*." Ms. Quinn wonders how to best respond. She wishes that English were simpler for beginning readers.

SHIFT

6

When Ms. Quinn pulls up next to Micah, he is beginning to reread yesterday's text. He flips the book open to the first page of text and takes off like a rocket, his eyes barely glancing at the words as he quickly recites, "A baby needs a bottle. A baby needs a diaper. A baby needs a book. A baby needs a blanket." Ms. Quinn stops him after the fourth page and says, "Let's go back. Use your finger to help you look more carefully at the words." Micah goes back to the first page and studies the words. He grins a bit when he sees that the first word is *the*, rather than *a*, both sight words that are familiar to him. He also deliberates over the word *his*, which he had read as *a*: "The baby needs a . . . /h/-/ĭ/-/s/, /h/-/ĭ/-/s/, his . . . . The baby needs his bottle." Ms. Quinn smiles and says, "You slowed down and blended all the way through that word, making every sound! Try the next page, slowing down to look carefully at the words." Sometimes Ms. Quinn worries that the predictable patterns in the beginning texts give students like Micah a false sense of success, when they have simply memorized the pattern.

As she glances up from Micah, Ms. Quinn notices that many of the students who are not at the small-group table are getting restless. Although she makes time for independent reading every day—no matter what—it seems to her that when she's not right there beside them, many of her students are just going through the motions. She is more and more concerned with how to provide her students with helpful and engaging experiences with text.

A COMMON PRACTICE TO RECONSIDER

▼ ▼ ▼ ▼ ▼ ▲

Overrelying on predictable texts to get kids quickly up and reading.

Chances are, if you are relying primarily on patterned texts to get students started as readers, you've experienced many of the same concerns as Ms. Quinn. When using beginning-level patterned texts, some emergent readers struggle to get started without elaborate text introductions or heavy-handed teaching of specific sight words (Burkins and Croft 2017 ; Burkins and Yaris 2016). Other students, like Micah, quickly memorize the sentence pattern and then seem to try to read on with barely a glance at the words. Still other children, like Farhia, put a great deal of effort into trying to draw from the print, but constantly encounter words they don't yet have the tools to decode.

Like us, maybe you find that there is a fine line between beginning texts that are too easy, requiring very little thinking or decoding, and those that are too hard, requiring orthographic work that is a complete mismatch for what students have learned in their phonics lessons. As balanced literacy teachers, we, like Ms. Quinn, believe wholeheartedly in teaching skills that are transferable to authentic reading. But what can we do about the disconnect between the skills in our phonics lessons and the words students encounter in their early reading texts? And how do we align our phonics instruction to our beginning reading texts when level A texts may have words like *umbrella*, *caterpillar*, and even *cereal*.

Clearing Up Some Confusion

You may be surprised to hear that we think one solution is to give decodable texts—those little books with a high percentage of regularly spelled words—a chance, both at the small-group table and during independent reading.

MISUNDERSTANDING:

Decodable texts are loaded with problems.

There's no question, decodable texts can be loaded with problems.

One big concern many teachers have with decodable texts and their controlled vocabulary is that they might teach children that reading *is not* a meaning-making endeavor. You've likely seen decodable texts whose narrow orthography results in unnatural language structures, tongue-twister effects, and boring or even nonsensical stories. Consider *A Red Pet*, in Figure 6.1.

Can Les get Ben a red pet?

Yes, you bet!

Figure 6.1 *A Red Pet*

But decodable texts for emergent readers are not the only beginning reading texts with limitations. Patterned texts have their own set of problems.

These highly predictable texts offer a different kind of controlled vocabulary, with patterns that exaggerate repeated words and phrases in ways that also come off sounding very little like everyday speech. They can also sometimes read like lists, providing limited opportunities for deep thinking (Burkins and Croft 2017; Burkins and Yaris 2016; Price-Mohr and Price 2020).

And when it comes to providing practice cracking our phonetic code, many patterned texts use words that may be decodable by definition but are not at all within the decoding reach of a beginning reader. To top it all off, the heavy support from the context, illustrations, and repetition often distract children from using the print, because they simply don't need to. Consider how the predictable B level text in Figure 6.2 would or wouldn't support a student in the partial alphabetic phase (see Table 4.3; Ehri 1995, 2002) who is working to build confidence with decoding CVC words.

Figure 6.2 *Children Can Play*

Put simply, finding texts we feel good about for the most beginning readers—texts with the right balance of interest, decodability, and opportunities for thought—is challenging work. However, these texts are definitely worth searching for, or even creating, to provide students ample, cumulative practice opportunities with texts that are both readable and engaging (Hatcher, Hulme, and Ellis 1994; Cheatham and Allor 2012; Blevins 2017; Moats and Tolman 2019).

So what can we do? Well, when selecting texts for beginning readers, there are at least three tensions to consider. We describe these tensions in the following sections and illustrate them in Figure 6.4.

Tension 1. Decodability Versus Predictability

Although all texts have some degree of predictability and decodability, there tends to be an inverse relationship between the two when it comes to beginning reading texts. To make texts more predictable, authors use more familiar and easily illustrated words, which often means using words that are less decodable. So a character in a highly predictable, or patterned, text may eat *spaghetti* rather than *meat*. On the other hand, many short but highly decodable words may be less familiar to children—*sob* versus *cry* and *ram* versus *sheep*.

Tension 2. Novelty Versus Repetition

Redundancy gives children multiple exposures to words. For example, patterned texts usually have a lot of repetition of high-frequency words. Decodable texts may also have word-level repetition, but they tend to have purposeful redundancy with particular sound-spelling patterns, such as lots of practice with a CVC pattern (*ran*, *sat*, and *cab*) or a vowel team (*ea* as in *bean*, *seat*, and *team*). *Novelty*, on the other hand, refers only to those unknown words built from familiar sound spellings (*cheek*, *seam*, *beach*).

Tension 3. Orthographic Value Versus Sense-making Value

A strong beginning reading text strikes a delicate balance between practicing known spelling patterns (orthographic value) and thinking about interesting ideas (sense-making value). Illustrations are an important tool for bridging this tension in beginning texts (Burkins and Croft 2017), potentially contributing to both cross-checking and sense-making.

Ultimately, the best texts for beginning readers offer a sweet spot between the competing demands of these three tensions. We refer to these as *aligned texts* because they align to the phonics instruction children are receiving, while also offering some element of contextual support *and* something to think about. Consider the text in Figure 6.3.

A pup can jump.

It can run.

A pup can run and jump.

Figure 6.3 *A Pup!*

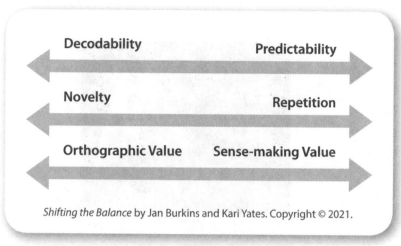

Shifting the Balance by Jan Burkins and Kari Yates. Copyright © 2021.

Figure 6.4 The Three Tensions in Beginning Reading Texts

You can use the three tensions in Figure 6.4 to evaluate any beginning reading text. We show examples of this in Figure 6.5 on page 142. Texts that fall toward the center indicate text characteristics that strike more of a balance between tensions and, therefore, are likely higher-quality selections for beginning readers. Texts that fall further toward the left or right are more imbalanced and probably less ideal.

Although we tend to talk about decodable texts and patterned texts as if the two are mutually exclusive, all texts have both decodability and predictability. Our work as teachers of beginning readers is to recognize when the decodability of texts and the ideas they represent match the learning needs of the reader; in other words, when the texts are *aligned* to needs of the reader.

 MISUNDERSTANDING:

Predictable texts make learning to read easier.

One of the perceived benefits of predictable texts is that they can help children start to feel and sound like fluent readers almost right from the start. Micah, for example, sounds like he's off to the races, which may seem exciting. However, he is barely glancing at the print, which is problematic.

Beginning readers are forming a hypothesis about how reading works. Without aligned texts readers are at risk of formulating the misguided hypothesis that reading is simply using the pictures, and maybe a few letters, to infer the words. Worse yet, readers like Micah, can begin to think that reading is really just memorizing the text.

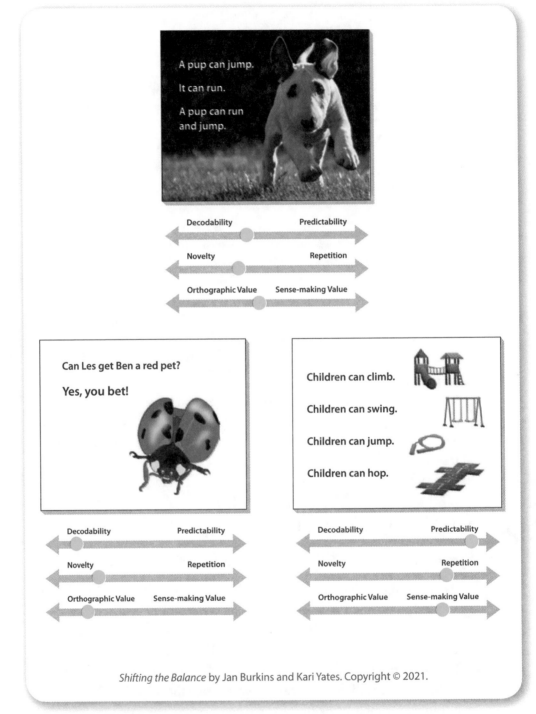

Figure 6.5 Evaluating Beginning Reading Texts with the Three Tensions

Of course, it *is* important to find a simple starting point for any complex learning task, but some of what we have done to create simple on-ramps to reading may carry some not-so-helpful consequences down the road.

Maximizing orthographic learning opportunities from the start requires texts that will give children reasons to slow down and look closely at print, even if this makes them sound less skilled for a little while (Doctor and Coltheart 1980; Harm and Seidenberg 2004).

The good news is that the crucial period of slow analysis should be temporary if children have sufficient practice with the print and continued parallel oral language development. Figure 6.6 illustrates the necessary peaks and predictable valley of becoming a reader who can truly focus on meaning because word recognition is effortless.

Remember Farhia, from the beginning of this chapter? She is a prime example of a student trying to sound out the words, laboring to apply what she's learned ("I like . . . /k/ . . . /k/ . . . crackers"), and still coming up short ("It looks like *cereal*, but *cereal* starts with /s/ like *snake*."). The use of patterned texts—loaded with many not-so-decodable-words—may be one reason saying

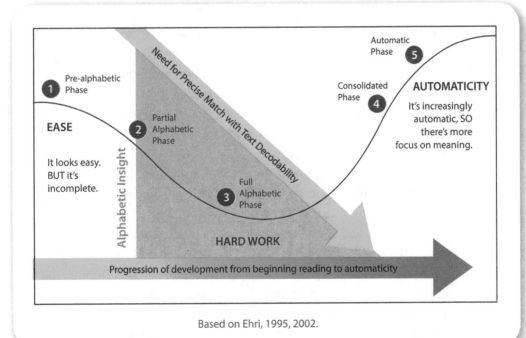

Based on Ehri, 1995, 2002.

Figure 6.6 Ease and Text Match Across Ehri's Phases

"sound it out" has seemed so unhelpful at times. By thoughtfully using texts with more aligned opportunities for decoding, we can show children, like Farhia, that the print *is* a reliable source of information, helping them learn to trust—rather than doubt—the alphabetic principle.

So, decodable texts, although initially requiring more effort, can serve as an important transitional tool that can help beginning readers use the power of print to move from the partial to the full alphabetic phase of word recognition (Ehri 2002; Moats and Tolman 2019). Excellent decodable texts can play a critical role in ensuring that students get lots of opportunities to use the new phonics they are learning (Juel and Roper-Schneider 1985; Blevins 2006, 2017).

MISUNDERSTANDING:

Using meaning as the go-to source of information will teach children to comprehend.

It seems logical to conclude that patterned texts do a better job of teaching children to comprehend than decodable texts, because children tend to spend less time working to decode these texts and presumably more time focused on meaning. However, there are serious limitations to the depth of the meaning or context work children can do in either patterned *or* decodable beginning reading texts. This is because both texts are necessarily built on content that is mostly familiar. So, although *both* patterned and decodable texts *can* offer meaning-making opportunities for novice readers—especially by including discussion-worthy illustrations—*neither* offers sufficiently deep value for reading comprehension growth.

We certainly don't want to wait, however, until children have sophisticated orthographic understandings to give them complex opportunities for sense-making! But if deep reading comprehension requires that children decode complex words and ideas, how do we *really* teach reading comprehension to young children?

The answer is—you guessed it—to teach comprehension through the oral language opportunities we talked about in Shift 1: read-aloud, shared reading, and classroom conversation. Until children can decode complex texts on their own, spoken language gives them a chance to practice thinking about complex ideas. It is a necessary complement to any use of beginning reading texts, whether decodable or patterned, serving as a placeholder for later comprehension work in more complex texts (Simple View of Reading).

So, what does this mean for instruction with those ubiquitous little books that are the backbone of so much beginning reading instruction? It means we shouldn't rely on them to carry too much of the weight of teaching children to comprehend. It also means that we're cautious not to assume that just because children understand their beginning reading texts, they will continue to comprehend as texts get more complex. Of course, meaningful conversation about the ideas in these little texts is certainly important, but we need to keep in mind that the most meaningful early work in comprehension happens in read-aloud, shared reading, and classroom conversation.

MISUNDERSTANDING:

As long as kids are spending time with books every day, they will become better readers.

We are strong advocates of both student choice and independent reading because we want students empowered to take charge of their own reading lives. High-volume independent reading—the idea that the more you read the better you get at reading—makes good common sense, has substantive research behind it (Stanovich 1986; Stanovich and West 1989; Anderson, Wilson, and Fielding 1988), and serves the ultimate goal of helping children become lifelong readers. After all, what is the purpose of investing all this time in phonemic awareness, systematic phonics, and orthographic mapping in the first place, if not to help readers harness it in the service of their own hopes and dreams as they develop rich and vibrant reading lives?

But much of the benefit of independent reading can be lost if students don't spend the majority of their time with texts that match their current skills as readers. Of course, even the most beginning readers can read trade literature, such as picture books and rich informational texts, in "other ways"—talking about illustrations and making up or retelling stories. But along with these other ways of reading, readers need lots of time with texts that set them up to "read all the words." After all, orthographic exposure that creates opportunities for self-teaching (Share 1995, 1999, 2004) is what strengthens children's neural pathways, making reading feel less like riding on a bumpy dirt road and more like zipping along a sophisticated superhighway.

Building orthographic superhighways requires readers to do more than just spend a lot of time *with* text. It requires that novice readers have lots of cumulative chances to prove and practice the current focus of their phonics instruction. One of the best ways to get this practice is by reading texts that are *aligned* to what they are learning. So, it's not just *how much* children are reading that matters, it is also *what* they are reading. Time in aligned texts, with orthographic patterns within a child's reach, leads to orthographic learning, rather than orthographic frustration, as Figure 6.7 illustrates.

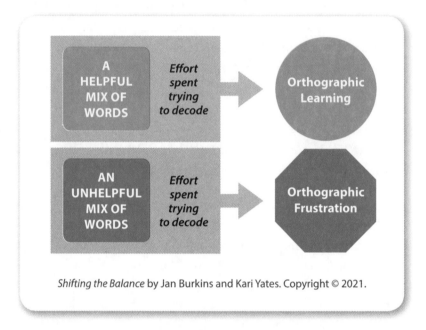

Shifting the Balance by Jan Burkins and Kari Yates. Copyright © 2021.

Figure 6.7 Formulas for Orthographic Learning and Orthographic Frustration

Remember in Shift 3 how we explored the complex nature of English's deep orthography? Well, children can't learn every bit of this through explicit phonics instruction. It is just too much and too complex. Luckily, they also learn about sound spellings as they engage in their own orthographic mapping on the run, or *self-teaching*, during independent reading (Share 1995, 1999, 2004).

Ensuring that beginning readers spend more time in aligned texts—or "read-all-the-words" texts—means they will need some guidance from you when it comes to selecting texts for independent reading. Because they are just learning the rules of the road for the alphabetic principle, we want their early travel experiences to shore up, rather than jumble, the early phonics principles they are working to internalize.

A Short Summary of the Science

▲ Both decodable texts and predictable texts have limitations.

▲ Selecting texts for beginning readers requires special attention to the text's decoding demands and how they align with what the child needs to practice.

▲ All texts are both decodable and predictable, to varying degrees.

▲ Although predictable texts may seem to make learning to read easier, they can create problems in the long run.

▲ Orthographic *learning* comes from effort spent decoding words composed of a mix of sound-spelling patterns aligned to what a student is learning.

▲ Orthographic *frustration* comes from expending effort trying to decode words made from sound-spellings children have not yet mastered.

▲ Neither predictable or decodable beginning reading texts teach children to comprehend well or deeply.

▲ Oral language experiences must supplement beginning reading texts to set children up for later success with comprehension in complex texts.

▲ High-volume reading from texts matched to children's developing print knowledge strengthens neural networks and makes word reading increasingly automatic.

6

THE SIMPLE AND SCIENTIFICALLY SOUND SHIFT

▼ ▼ ▼ ▼ ▼ ▲

Thoughtfully select or create texts with the decoding opportunities students need to practice.

Recommendations for Making the Shift

The challenge of consistently finding (or creating) beginning reading texts that have both aligned orthographic learning opportunities and engaging content is tricky at best. In the recommendations that follow, we offer suggestions to support you as you find, evaluate, and use beginning reading texts for both sense-making and decoding.

Learn to use a few high-leverage routines for sharing aligned texts with students.

In Table 6.1, we describe some routines for finding, evaluating, and even creating engaging beginning reading texts that align with the sound spellings beginning readers are learning. We also offer recommendations for supporting students' independent reading, both with aligned texts and with trade books. In the sections that follow, we zoom in on each of the routines in Table 6.1.

TABLE 6.1

HIGH-LEVERAGE INSTRUCTIONAL ROUTINES FOR TEXT CHOICE

The What: *Routine*	The Why: *Purpose*
Evaluate texts.	To engage in a process for thoughtfully considering the characteristics of beginning reading texts
Write aligned texts.	To develop comfort with composing your own texts—aligned to specific phonics principles and high-frequency words—for use across the learning day
Use patterned texts in better ways.	To develop new practices for the use of patterned texts, minimizing their drawbacks and maximizing alphabetic principle, orthographic learning, and sense-making
Honor multiple ways to read.	To develop independent reading practices that support both sides of the Simple View of Reading equation by providing children "read-all-the-words" texts (best for decoding practice and building orthographic learning) *and* "read-in-other-ways" texts (best for sense-making and oral language development)
Support book choice.	To support student book choice for independent reading, ensuring students have texts in which they can read the words *and* texts they might read in other ways

6

Zooming In on Evaluating Texts

To let go of thinking about texts as either decodable or patterned, we encourage you to practice using the three tensions to analyze the features of emergent-level texts and decide which are a match for your students. This can be fun and informative work. Invite a colleague or your whole team to sit down and experiment with the tool, to learn from each other and calibrate your thinking. Use the questions in Figure 6.8 to help you consider where individual texts fall along these continuums. If you'd like a copy to jot notes on as you evaluate texts, you can get it at **TheSixShifts.com**/downloadables.

Other important questions for evaluating how well a beginning reading text will match a reader's skills include:

▲ How natural sounding is the language structure for the students for students?

▲ What high-frequency words will the readers need to know?

▲ How do the illustrations connect to the words? Do they deepen the story or information? Will they supplant decoding words?

Decodability	Predictability
How regular are the words in the text?	Do the pattern and/or the illustrations make the words easy to predict?
Novelty	Repetition
Will children encounter new words built from familiar sound-spellings?	Are words or spelling patterns repeated to give students practice with them?
Orthographic Value	Sense-making Value
How aligned is the text to the reader's current phonics knowledge/learning?	Does the text make sense? Does the text engage the reader in thinking?

Shifting the Balance by Jan Burkins and Kari Yates. Copyright © 2021.

Figure 6.8 Questions for Using the Three Tensions

In addition to these specifics, there are important global factors to consider such as, who does the text represent and who is left out? Consider racial, cultural, socioeconomic, gender, and other types of diversity, as well student interest in the topic and ways it may be relevant to the reader.

There are very few, if any, perfect texts for beginning readers. Yet learning to look critically at every text so that you understand the advantages and pitfalls within it can be enlightening. We invite you to take this work even one step further: not only evaluating texts but also doing the hard work of eliminating those that just don't serve readers well enough.

 ## Zooming In on Writing Aligned Texts

Whatever skills you are teaching in your phonics lesson on a given day, you will want to weave in opportunities for your students to reencounter them in print as often as possible and in a variety of settings across the days that follow. You don't have to buy all the texts you need, however. Equipped with your phonics progression and a prioritized high-frequency word list, you can create simple aligned texts that can give students some of the practice they need. You can embed the texts you create into morning messages, shared reading, dictation, independent reading, and even send them home. There are a number of ways to approach this creative process. In Table 6.2, we list simple steps that have worked for us.

TABLE 6.2

A PROCESS FOR WRITING ALIGNED TEXTS

Process	Example
Identify phonics principles. Refer to your scope and sequence, or keep a running list of the sound/spelling patterns you've taught, including those that are familiar and those that are new.	Children are learning to decode CVC words with /ĭ/. They've had previous practice reading words with the vowel sounds /ă/, /ŏ/, and /ŭ/.
Choose a few key high-frequency words. Consult your prioritized list of high-frequency words. Identify words children know, words they are learning, and words that are regularly spelled with already learned sound spellings.	Children know most of the first thirteen high-frequency words. They recently engaged in orthographic mapping of the word *have* during interactive writing.

continues

Process	Example
Choose a topic. Select a subject or a story line that is relevant for your students. Browsing images may be helpful.	Recent rain has resulted in lots of mud on the playground. The mud is a definite attraction for children.
Compose the text. Craft your text, considering decodability, predictability, novelty, repetition, orthographic value, and sense-making value.	We play in the mud. We hop. We slip. We have fun. Mom gets mad!
Add interest with electronic images. If you want your text to have an illustration, go to a free image site, such as pixabay.com, and look for an image that would be interesting for children. Be thoughtful about who is represented in the images you choose.	

Of course, writing is not a linear process. Sometimes when we craft aligned texts, we begin by looking for images to help us choose a subject. Other times, we begin with a phonics principle and look for words around which we can build a text. Still other times, we start with a subject that we know interests the students. So, experiment with rearranging the steps in the process and make it your own.

A word of caution: image sites are not typically diverse in representations of people, and it is easy to overlook this systemic problem when you are focused on finding a particular image to illustrate an idea. Putting in the extra work to find illustrations that show diversity is an important way to honor and validate all children.

Zooming In on Using Patterned Texts in Better Ways

The problems with patterned text do not mean that you need to throw them all out—although you may find you want to get rid of some of them. At the very least, we hope you will begin to look at them differently now. Like decodable texts, however, some patterned texts are better than others. Once you have narrowed your patterned texts to the best of your collection, you're ready to revise the ways you use them.

Here are a few things to keep in mind when using patterned texts with children:

▲ Teach children to deliberately use the print (Burkins and Croft 2017), even in a patterned text, which is designed to attract students' first attention to context. Be consistent in prompting students to try decoding first, as we described in Shift 5. This can help offset the ways that repetitive language patterns inhibit the use of orthographic information.

▲ Words that are beyond the scope of a reader's decoding skill, but clearly supported by the illustrations, are often great words for the orthographic mapping procedure (page 104) or for taking to writing (page 127). Because this analysis interrupts reading and takes a few minutes, it's important to use these strategies sparingly, however. We suggest no more than one or two words per book.

▲ Consider the accessible decoding opportunities a patterned text offers, and be sure you don't inadvertently make the work too easy through an overly comprehensive book walk or heavy introduction (Burkins and Croft 2017; Burkins and Yaris 2016).

▲ Levels A and B patterned texts can play an important role in helping children solidify the core of the alphabetic principle, as well as other critical concepts about print such as one-to-one matching of spoken words to printed words. But the more aligned and considerate the words (*rain* vs. *thunderstorm*) in the A or B text, the more likely they are to help readers' emerging understandings of sound-symbol correspondences take root. So, these first books especially need extra scrutiny.

Zooming In on Honoring Multiple Ways to Read

To ensure that the most beginning readers develop proficiency in both sides of the Simple View of Reading equation—word reading and listening comprehension—young readers really need daily interactions with both types of texts:

▲ aligned beginning reading texts in which they can read all the words, and

▲ rich trade literature they can read in other ways.

These two types of texts serve different but parallel purposes. Table 6.3 describes both, their uses, and their value.

TABLE 6.3

TWO KINDS OF INDEPENDENT READING TEXTS FOR BEGINNING READERS

	"Read-All-the-Words" Texts (Aligned Texts)	"Read-in-Other-Ways" Texts (Trade Literature)
What it mostly looks like	Children read all of the words on the page. The work may look deliberate or slow. Children may point to words and will probably reread words and sentences as they figure them out.	Children study and "read" the pictures. Children talk with friends about the text and may participate in collaborative retellings.
What else might children do with these books?	Children may also notice and talk about the illustrations and story/ information.	Children may also notice the print and attempt to decode some words.
Why it's important	Children strengthen their understanding of the alphabetic principle. They decode, self-teach, accumulate orthographic knowledge, and grow to love reading.	Children engage with familiar and new texts, practicing and extending oral language. They enjoy a wide range of books and grow to love reading.
Who chooses the texts?	Teacher chooses some texts. For other texts, choice is scaffolded or narrowed by the teacher.	Students choose from a wide variety of trade literature in the classroom or school library. Student choice is not limited.

Here are a few tips for translating the items in Table 6.3 into classroom practice:

▲ Provide an extra baggie to help students separate "read-all-the-words" books from "read-in-other-ways" books.

▲ Let the "read-all-the-words" books that children have read during small-group instruction serve as seed books in this extra baggie. The obvious advantage here is that you already know these texts are a match for the reader. In addition to these guided reading books, you can choose other aligned texts for, or even with, your students. (We offer suggestions for supported book selection in the next section.)

▲ When all of your students are reading independently at once, you can make sure they get time with both types of texts by having them start with their "read-all-the-words" books. When they hear a signal or you call time, let them decide if they wish to continue with their aligned texts or shift to texts they can read in other ways.

▲ If your students are choosing independent reading at different times during the literacy block, you can teach them to do a read-through of all the books in their separate "read-all-the-words" baggies before going on to other types of reading.

Of course, "read-all-the-words" and "read-in-other-ways" texts are not complete opposites. Children may talk about and otherwise develop oral language when they work in their decodable and beginning reading texts. They may also find opportunities to look at the print and decode in predictable and trade books. It makes sense to be flexible and creative as you bring this shift to life.

Zooming In on Supported Book Choice

If your students currently choose *all* of their own texts for independent reading, you may want to make space for more teacher-supported text selection, particularly with "read-all-the-words" texts. These revisions to your book-shopping process are especially critical for students reading in kindergarten through mid-first-grade levels. Next, we offer four suggestions for teacher-supported book shopping.

▲ Rather than just turning students loose to choose texts for independent reading, use small-group instruction or conferring (Yates and Nosek 2018) to support students as they refresh their independent reading choices each week.

▲ Choice doesn't have to mean limitless choice. So, you might try offering a smaller selection of beginning reader titles to an individual or small group, saying something like, "These are some books I'm excited to share with you! Let me tell you a bit about them so that you can pick the ones you'd like to read."

▲ Don't have students trade out all of their "read-all-the-words" books for new texts at once (Yates 2015). This can create a next-day disaster as beginning readers find themselves faced with all new, and no familiar, texts. Instead, consider having students trade about half of their texts each week. Say something like, "Choose four texts you'd like to exchange, and then let's look together at some new options."

▲ Create duplicate copies of familiar texts that you have used or created in different instructional contexts. For instance, give everyone their own copy of shared reading texts for repeated reading practice, or bind morning messages into a book to keep in the classroom library.

▼ ▼ ▼ ▼ ▼ ▲

Meanwhile, Back in the Classroom . . .

Committed to making the most of independent reading practices in her classroom, Ms. Quinn decides to make some changes. To begin, she gives each child a curated baggie of books for them to keep inside their individual box of self-selected titles. Each baggie has a few seed books for each child, carefully chosen by Ms. Quinn. Some are new leveled texts, and some are texts that are already familiar from guided reading sessions.

Next, she helps her young readers learn a new routine for independent reading. The new routine has them start each independent reading session with their baggie of "read-all-the-words" texts. Then, when Ms. Quinn sounds the chimes, they are free to move on to their self-selected "read-in-other-ways" texts, if they want to.

The trickiest part of the new routine seems to be finding enough considerate texts that are truly aligned to her phonics instruction to offer her students the orthographic learning opportunities they need.

But today, Ms. Quinn is excited as she makes her way to the guided reading book room. A few weeks back, the literacy coach purchased a new infusion of beginning reading texts for guided reading, and they are ready for checkout! Anxious for some fresh titles to share with her children and tired of trying to recycle titles, she is really looking forward to exploring these new books.

Upon arrival, however, she is surprised to discover the new titles are not on the shelves with the leveled texts. Instead, the literacy coach has set them up on a table with a sign reading, "New decodables for beginning readers!" Ms. Quinn finds this interesting, because this same literacy coach has previously expressed hesitations about decodable texts. Other decodable texts live in closets or the top shelf of the library storage room because no one is interested in them.

In a previous district Ms. Quinn had been required to use a series of primitive-looking decodables made from blackline masters. They all read like tongue twisters—*Min and Jin sit in a tin!*—and her children were confused by them. They left her with a real distaste for decodable texts. Because she trusts the coach and is eager to nudge her students forward, she decides to take a look, despite feeling some skepticism.

As she starts to page through a few of the little books, she is immediately struck by how truly beautiful they are. All have bright engaging pictures, diverse characters, and interesting settings. She feels herself relax a bit, opening up to possibilities.

Another thing she notices is that—much like the decodables of her past— the earliest texts in this set are chock full of CVC words. But what strikes her as different about these books is that the story lines make more sense and the language is not tongue twisting. She finds herself thinking about specific students, like Farhia, who is baffled when the print does not reliably draw on the entry-level sound-spelling relationships she knows. "Farhia would probably be able to read these books," she thinks to herself.

The next thing that strikes Ms. Quinn is that these texts do not rely heavily on a predictable pattern. Instead, they have varied sentence structures from page to page. She reflects on how Micah's strong oral language sometimes seems to get in the way of looking carefully at the words in patterned texts. She thinks Micah might just engage with these texts more completely. The illustrations and story lines will pull him in, but he won't be able to avoid looking closely at the words.

Ms. Quinn chooses four sets of the decodable texts to take back to her classroom, excited to see how her students respond to them.

Questions for Reflection

Current Texts: What types of texts do you currently use with beginning readers? Patterned? Decodable? A mix of both?

Benefits and Barriers: What are the advantages and limitations of the texts you are currently using? How can you use the texts differently to offset those limitations?

Text Evaluation: How might you utilize the three tensions—decodability versus predictability, novelty versus repetition, orthographic value versus sense-making value—to analyze the texts you share with beginning readers?

Diversity: How well does your collection of texts provide diverse representations of race, socioeconomics, gender, socioculture, and more?

Writing Texts: What opportunities might you have for creating decodable texts for your students? Morning message? Interactive writing? Short paragraphs or texts?

Book Room: What type of texts might you advocate for adding to your school's book room or classroom collection?

Text Choice: What adjustments might you make to ensure more access to both aligned texts and excellent trade literature? How might you change your book-choosing routines to ensure part of independent reading time is spent with aligned texts?

Putting It All Together: How do the ideas in this shift connect back to each of the previous shifts? How does thoughtful text selection support implementation of all of the shifts in this book?

AFTERWORD

Dear Readers,

For some of you, perhaps the ideas in this book validated your ever-evolving thinking about teaching children to read. For others, maybe what you've read in these pages disrupted your mental model for balanced literacy. It may have rattled you and left you questioning some of what you've held dear. It may even have left you wishing you had done some things differently in the past. We understand all of these emotions—more than a little bit—because this work has put us in the same uncomfortable places.

In fact, deciding to write this book wasn't easy. There were a lot of good reasons *not* to.

We aren't researchers and we aren't scientists. The topic is enormous and controversial and complex. To do it justice we knew we'd have to write some things that made us uncomfortable. We would have to question things we'd written and taught in the past. We would have to write things people on both sides were bound to have strong opinions about. And we worried that trying to bridge the gap between science and balance would leave us in a lonely middle. Not to mention there was a global pandemic going on.

But we did decide to write it after all. And now you've read it.

So, what really matters next is what you will do as you teach the readers in front of you tomorrow.

Perhaps you are curious to try out some of these ideas. If so, we invite you to pick one of the shifts and roll up your sleeves. Maybe you'll choose the shift that seems most urgent for you. Maybe you'll choose the one that seems most manageable. There's really no wrong place to start. Just make an action plan with steps for today, tomorrow, next week, and even next month. Pay attention to your energy as you go, and be kind to yourself along the way.

As vulnerable as this project has made us feel at times, we definitely wouldn't have wanted to do it alone. Likewise, you might consider inviting a friend to join you on your journey. Together, you may choose to download the study guide (Stenhouse.com/ShiftingtheBalance). Our reference section on the next few pages will offer ideas for more reading, or you can visit our website, **TheSixShifts.com**, for recommended titles. We'll meet you there, to continue the conversation.

With love,

Jan and Kari

We are @TheSixShifts on Facebook, Instagram, and Twitter. You can also contact us through our website, TheSixShifts.com, directly.

REFERENCES

Adams, Marilyn J. 1990. *Beginning to Read: Thinking and Learning About Print.* Cambridge, MA: MIT Press.

——. 1998. "The Three-Cueing System." In *Literacy for All: Issues in Teaching and Reading*, ed. Jean Osborn and Fran Lehr. New York: Guilford.

Adlof, Suzanne M., Hugh W. Catts, and Todd D. Little. 2006. "Should the Simple View of Reading Include a Fluency Component?" *Reading and Writing* 19 (9): 933–958. doi: 10.1007/s11145-006-9024-z.

Anderson, Richard C., Paul T. Wilson, and Linda G. Fielding. 1988. "Growth in Reading and How Children Spend Their Time Outside of School." *Reading Research Quarterly* 23 (3): 285–303. doi: 10.1598/rrq.23.3.2.

Beck, Isabel L., and Mark E. Beck. 2013. *Making Sense of Phonics: The Hows and Whys.* New York: Guilford.

Berninger, Virginia W., and Todd L. Richards. 2002. *Brain Literacy for Educators and Psychologists.* Amsterdam, The Netherlands: Academic.

Blachman, Benita A. 1991. "Getting Ready to Read: Learning How Print Maps to Speech." In *The Language Continuum: From Infancy to Literacy*, ed. J. F. Kavanagh (pp. 41–62). Timonium, MD: York.

——. 1995. *Identifying the Core Linguistic Deficits and the Critical Conditions for Early Intervention with Children with Reading Disabilities.* Paper presented at the annual meeting of the Learning Disabilities Association, Orlando, FL, March 1995.

——. 2000. "Phonological Awareness." In *Handbook of Reading Research*, 3rd ed., ed. M. L. Kamil, P. B. Rosenthal, P. D. Pearson, and R. Barr (pp. 483–502). Mahwah, NJ: Erlbaum.

Blevins, Wiley. 2006. *Phonics from A–Z: A Practical Guide.* New York: Scholastic.

——. 2017. *A Fresh Look at Phonics: Common Causes of Failure and 7 Ingredients for Success.* Thousand Oaks, CA: Corwin.

Bowers, Jeffrey S., and Peter N. Bowers. 2017. "Beyond Phonics: The Case for Teaching Children the Logic of the English Spelling System." *Educational Psychologist* 52 (2): 124-141. doi: 10.1080/00461520.2017.1288571

Brady, Susan. 1986. "Short-Term Memory, Phonological Processing, and Reading Ability." *Annals of Dyslexia* 36 (1): 138–153. doi:10.1007/BF02648026.

Brady, Susan. (2020). "A 2020 Perspective on Research Findings on Alphabetics (Phoneme Awareness and Phonics): Implications for Instruction." *The Reading League Journal* 1 (3): 20–28.

———. January 2020. "Strategies Used in Education for Resisting the Evidence and Implications of the Science of Reading." *The Reading League Journal* 1 (1): 33–40.

Burkins, Jan, and Melody Croft. 2017. *Preventing Misguided Reading: Next Generation Guided Reading Strategies.* Portsmouth, NH: Stenhouse.

Burkins, Jan, and Kim Yaris. 2016. *Who's Doing the Work? How to Say Less So Readers Can Do More.* Portsmouth, NH: Stenhouse.

Bus, Adriana G., and Marinus H. van IJzendoorn. 1999. "Phonological Awareness and Early Reading: A Meta-Analysis of Experimental Training Studies." *Journal of Educational Psychology* 91 (3): 403–414. doi:10.1037/00220663.91.3.403.

Byrne, Brian. 2005. "Theories of Learning to Read." In *The Science of Reading: A Handbook,* eds. M. J. Snowling and C. Hulme (pp. 104-119). Malden, MA: Bladwell. doi: 10.1002/9780470757642.ch6.

Byrne, Brian, and Ruth Fielding-Barnsley. 1989. "Phonemic Awareness and Letter Knowledge in the Child's Acquisition of the Alphabetic Principle." *Journal of Educational Psychology* 81 (3): 313–321. doi:10.1037/0022-0663.81.3.313.

Carroll, John B., Peter Davies, and Barry Richman. 1971. *Word Frequency Book.* Boston: Houghton Mifflin.

Castles, Anne, and Max Coltheart. 2004. "Is There a Causal Link from Phonological Awareness to Success in Learning to Read?" *Cognition* 91 (1): 77–111. doi:10.1016/s0010-0277(03)00164-1.

Castles, Anne, Max Coltheart, Katherine R. Wilson, Jodie Valpied, and Joanne Wedgwood. 2009. "The Genesis of Reading Ability: What Helps Children Learn Letter–Sound Correspondences?" *Journal of Experimental Child Psychology* 104 (1): 68–88. doi:10.1016/j.jecp.2008.12.003.

Castles, Anne, and Kate Nation. 2006. "How Does Orthographic Learning Happen?" In *From Inkmarks to Ideas: Current Issues in Lexical Processing,* ed. S. Andrews (pp. 151–179). Hove, England: Psychology Press.

Castles, Anne, Kathleen Rastle, and Kate Nation. 2018. "Ending the Reading Wars: Reading Acquisition from Novice to Expert." *Psychological Science in the Public Interest* 19 (1): 5–51. doi: 10.11/77/1529100618772271.

Catts, Hugh W., Suzanne Adlof, and Susan Ellis-Weismer. 2006. "Language Deficits in Poor Comprehenders: A Case for the Simple View of Reading." *Journal of Speech, Language, and Hearing Research* 49 (2): 278–293. doi:10.1044/1092-4388(2006/023).

Catts, Hugh W., Tiffany P. Hogan, and Suzanne M. Adlof. 2005. "Developmental Changes in Reading and Reading Disabilities." In *The Connections Between Language and Reading Disabilities*, ed. H. W. Catts and A. G. Kamhi (pp. 25–40). Mahwah, NJ: Lawrence Erlbaum.

Cervettie, Gina N., P. David Pearson, Peter Afflerbach, Panayiota Kendeou, Gina Biancarosa, Jennifer Higgs, Miranda S. Fitzgerald, and Amy I. Berman. 2020. "How the Reading for Understanding Initiative's Research Complicates the Simple View of Reading Invoked in the Science of Reading." *Reading Research Quarterly* 55 (S1): S161-S172. doi:10.1002/rrq.343.

Cheatham, Jennifer P., and Jill H. Allor. 2012. "The Influence of Decodability in Early Reading Text on Reading Achievement: A Review of the Evidence." *Reading and Writing: An Interdisciplinary Journal* 25 (9): 2223–2246. https://eric.ed.gov/?id=EJ979471.

Cisneros, Sandra. 1994. *La Casa en Mango Street.* New York: Vintage Español.

Clay, Marie M. 1993. *Reading Recovery: A Guidebook for Teachers in Training.* Portsmouth, NH: Heinemann.

———. 2013. *An Observation Survey of Early Literacy Achievement*, 3rd ed. Portsmouth, NH: Heinemann.

———. 2015. *Becoming Literate: The Construction of Inner Control.* Portsmouth, NH: Heinemann.

———. 2016. *Literacy Lessons Designed for Individuals*, 2nd ed. Portsmouth, NH: Heinemann.

———. 2017. *Running Records for Classroom Teachers*, 2nd ed. Portsmouth, NH. Heinemann.

Cohen, Laurent, Stanislas Dehaene, Lionel Naccache, Stéphane Lehéricy, Ghislaine Dehaene-Lambertz, Marie-Anne Hénaff, and François Michel. 2000. "The Visual Word Form Area: Spatial and Temporal Characterization of an Initial Stage of Reading in Normal Subjects and Posterior Split-brain Patients." *Brain* 123 (2): 291–307. doi:10.1093/brain/123.2.291.

Coltheart, Max, Kathleen Rastle, Conrad Perry, Robyn Langdon, and Johannes Ziegler. 2001. "DRC: A Dual Route Cascaded Model of Visual Word Recognition and Reading Aloud." *Psychological Review* 108 (1): 204–256. doi: 10.1037//0033-295x.108.1.204.

Cooney, John B., and H. Lee Swanson. 1987. "Memory and Learning Disabilities: An Overview." In *Memory and Learning Disabilities: Advances in Learning and Behavioral Disabilities*, ed. H. L. Swanson (pp. 1–40). Greenwich, CT: JAI.

Clayton, Francina J., Gillian West, Claire Sears, Chalres Hulme, and Arne Lervåg. 2020. "A Longitudinal Study of Early Reading Development: Letter-Sound Knowledge, Phoneme Awareness and RAN, but Not Letter-Sound Integration, Predict Variations in Reading Development." *Scientific Studies of Reading* 24 (2): 91-107. https://doi.org/10.1080/10888438.2019.1622546

Curtis, Mary E. 1980. "Development of Components of Reading Skill." *Journal of Educational Psychology* 72 (5): 656-669. https://doi.org/10.1037/0022-0663.72.5.656

DeCasper, Anthony J., and Melanie J. Spence. 1986. "Prenatal Maternal Speech Influences Newborns' Perception of Speech Sounds." *Infant Behavior and Development* 9 (2): 133-150. doi: 10.1016/0163-6383(86)90025-1.

Dehaene, Stanislas. 2009. *Reading in the Brain: The New Science of How We Read.* New York: Penguin Group.

———. 2013. "Inside the Letter Box: How Literacy Transforms the Human Brain." *Cerebrum* 7 (2013): 1–16. https://www.ncbi.nlm.nih.gov/pmc/articles/PMC3704307/.

Dehaene, Stanislas, Kimihio Nakamura, Antoinette Jobert, Chihiro Kuroki, Seiji Ogawa, and Laurent Cohen. 2010. "Why Do Children Make Mirror Errors in Reading? Neural Correlates of Mirror Invariance in the Visual Word Form Area." *Neuroimage* 49 (2): 1837–1848. doi: 10.1016/j.neuroimage.2009.09.024.

Delpit, Lisa. 2012. *"Multiplication Is for White People": Raising Expectations for Other People's Children.* New York: The New Press.

Doctor, Estelle Anne, and Max Coltheart. 1980. "Children's Use of Phonological Encoding When Reading for Meaning." *Memory and Cognition* 8 (3): 195–209. doi:10.3758/BF03197607.

Dreyer, Lois G., and Leonard Katz. 1992. "An Examination of the 'Simple View of Reading.'" *Haskins Laboratories Status Report on Speech Research SR-1l1/112: 169–176.* http://www.haskins.yale.edu/sr/SR111/SR111_12.pdf.

Duke, Nell K., and Heidi Anne E. Mesmer. 2018. "Phonics Faux Pas: Avoiding Instructional Missteps in Teaching Letter Sound Relationships." *American Educator* 42 (4): 12–16.

Dweck, Carol. 2017. *Mindset: Changing the Way You Think to Fulfill Your Potential.* New York: Random House.

Dyson, Hannah, Wendy Best, Jonathan Solity, and Charles Hulme. 2017. "Training Mispronunciation Correction and Word Meanings Improves Children's Ability to Learn to Read Words." *Scientific Studies of Reading* 21 (5): 392–407. doi:10.1080/10888438.2017.1315424.

Elbro, Carsten. 1996. "Early Linguistic Abilities and Reading Development: A Review and a Hypothesis." *Reading and Writing: An Interdisciplinary Journal* 8 (6): 453–485. doi: 10.1007/BF00577023.

Elbro, Carsten, and Peter F. de Jong. 2017. "Orthographic Learning Is Verbal Learning: The Role of Spelling Mispronunciations." In *Theories of Reading Development*, ed. K. Cain, D. Compton, and R. Parrila (pp. 148–168). Amsterdam, The Netherlands: John Benjamins.

Ehri, Linnea C. 1995. "Phases of Development in Learning to Read Words by Sight." *Journal of Research in Reading* 18 (2): 116–125. doi: 10.1111/j.1467-9817.1995.tb00077.x.

———. 1998. "Grapheme-Phoneme Knowledge Is Essential for Learning to Read Words in English." In *Word Recognition in Beginning Literacy*, ed. J. L. Metsala and L. C. Ehri (pp. 3–40). Mahwah, NJ: Earlbaum.

———. 2002. "Phases of Acquisition in Learning to Read Words and Implications for Teaching." In *Learning and Teaching Reading*, ed. R. Stainthorp and P. Tomlinson (pp. 7–28). *British Journal of Educational Psychology Monograph Series II: Part 1*. London: British Journal of Educational Psychology.

———. 2005a. "Learning to Read Words: Theory, Findings, and Issues." *Scientific Studies of Reading* 9 (2): 167–188. doi: 10.1207/s1532799xssr0902_4.

———. 2005b. "Development of Sight Word Reading: Phases and Findings." In *The Science of Reading: A Handbook*, ed. M. J. Snowling and C. Hume (pp. 135–154). Oxford, UK: Blackwell.

———. 2014. "Orthographic Mapping in the Acquisition of Sight Word Reading, Spelling Memory, and Vocabulary Learning." *Scientific Studies of Reading* 18 (1): 5–21.

———. 2017. "Orthographic Mapping and Literacy Development Revisited." In *Theories of Reading Development*, ed. K. Cain, D. L. Compton, and R. K. Parrila (pp. 169–190). Amsterdam, The Netherlands: John Benjamins. doi:10.1075/swll.15.08ehr.

Ehri, Linnea C., Simone R. Nunes, Dale M. Willows, Barbara Valeska Schuster, Zohreh Yaghoub-Zadeh, and Timothy Shanahan. 2001. "Systematic Phonics Instruction Helps Students Learn to Read: Evidence from the National Reading Panel's Meta-Analysis." *Reading* 36 (3): 250–287. doi:10.3102/00346543071003393.

Elkonin, Daniil B. 1973. "Methods of Teaching Reading." In *Comparative Reading: Cross National Studies of Behavior and Processing in Reading and Writing*, ed. J. Downing (pp. 551–579). New York: McMillan.

Fountas, Irene, and Gay Su Pinnell. 2008. *Fountas and Pinnell Prompting Guide, Part 1 for Oral Reading and Early Writing*. Portsmouth, NH. Heinemann.

Fountas, Irene, and Gay Su Pinnell. 2009. *When Readers Struggle: Teaching That Works*. Portsmouth, NH: Heinemann.

Fountas, Irene, and Gay Su Pinnell. 2016. *Guided Reading: Responsive Teaching Across the Grades*, 2nd ed. Portsmouth, NH. Heinemann.

Fry, Edward. 1980. "The New Instant Word List." *The Reading Teacher* 34 (3): 284–289.

Galuschka, K., E. Ise, K. Krick, and G. Schulte-Korne. 2014. "Effectiveness of Treatment Approaches for Children and Adolescents with Reading Disabilities: A Meta-Analysis of Randomized Controlled Trials." *PLoS One* 9 (2): Article e89900. doi:10.1371/journal.pone.0089900.

Gentry, J. Richard, and Gene P. Ouellette. 2019. *Brain Words: How the Science of Reading Informs Teaching*. Portsmouth, NH: Stenhouse.

Gough, Philip B., Jack A. Alford, and Pamela Holley-Wilcox. "Words and Contexts." *Perception of Print* 28, (1981): 85–100.

Gough, Philip B., and William E. Tunmer. 1986. "Decoding, Reading, and Reading Disability." *Remedial and Special Education* 7 (1): 6–10. doi: 10.1177/074193258600700104.

Gough, Philip B., and S. A. Wren. 1998. "The Decomposition of Decoding." In *Reading and Spelling: Development and Disorders*, eds. C. Hulme and R. Joshi (pp. 19-32). Malwah, NJ: Lawrence Earlbaum Associates.

Graesser, Arthur C., Murray Singer, and Tom Trabasso. 1994. "Constructing Inferences During Narrative Text Comprehension." *Psychological Review* 101 (3): 371. doi: 10.1037/0033-295X.101.3.371.

Hanford, Emily. August 6, 2020. "What the Words Say: Many Kids Struggle With Reading—and Children of Color are Far Less Likely to Get the Help They Need." American Public Media Reports (Online Article): https://www.apmreports.org/episode/2020/08/06/what-the-words-say?utm_campaign=APM+Reports+-+Reading+Comprehension+-+20200806_100717&utm_medium=email&utm_source=sfmc_Newsletter&utm_content=reading%20comprehension&utm_term=3732367

Hanford, Emily. September 10, 2018. "Hard Words: Why Aren't Our Kids Being Taught to Read?" American Public Media Reports (Online Article): https://www.apmreports.org/episode/2018/09/10/hard-words-why-american-kids-arent-being-taught-to-read

Hargrave, Anne C., and Monique Sénéchal. 2000. "A Book Reading Intervention with Preschool Children Who Have Limited Vocabularies: The Benefits of Regular Reading and Dialogic Reading." *Early Childhood Research Quarterly* 15 (1): 75–90.

Harm, Michael W., and Mark S. Seidenberg. 2004. "Computing the Meanings of Words in Reading: Cooperative Division of Labor Between Visual and Phonological Processes." *Psychological Review* 111 (3): 662–720. doi:10.1037/0033-295X.111.3.662.

Hatcher, Peter. J., Charles Hulme, and Andrew W. Ellis. 1994. "Ameliorating Early Reading Failure by Integrating the Teaching of Reading and Phonological Skills: The Phonological Linkage Hypothesis." *Child Development* 65 (1): 41–57. doi:10.1111/j.1467-8624.1994.tb00733.x.

Hogan, Tiffany P., Suzanne M. Adlof, and Crystle N. Alonzo. 2014. "On the Importance of Listening Comprehension." *International Journal of Speech-Language Pathology* 16 (3): 199–207. doi: 10.3109/17549507.2014.904441.

Hoover, Wesley A., and Philip B. Gough. 1990. "The Simple View of Reading." *Reading and Writing* 2 (2): 127–160.

Hulme, Charles, Claudia Bowyer-Crane, Julia M. Carroll, Fiona J. Duff, and Margaret J. Snowling. 2012. "The Causal Role of Phoneme Awareness and Letter-Sound Knowledge in Learning to Read: Combining Intervention Studies with Mediation Analyses." *Psychological Science* 23 (6): 572–577. doi:10.1177/0956797611435921.

Johns, Jerry L. 1980. "First Graders' Concepts About Print." *Reading Research Quarterly* 15 (4): 529–549. doi: 10.2307/747278.

Johnston, R S., S McGeown, and J E. Watson. 2012. "Long-Term Effects of Synthetic Versus Analytic Phonics Teaching on the Reading and Spelling Ability of 10-Year-Old Boys and Girls." *Reading and Writing* 25: 1365–1384. doi: 10.1007/s11145-011-9323-x.

Joshi, R. Malatesha, and P. G. Aaron. 2000. "The Component Model of Reading: Simple View of Reading Made a Little More Complex." *Reading Psychology* 21 (2): 85–97. Also available online at https://www.researchgate.net/publication/233617523_The_component_model_of_reading_Simple_view_of_reading_made_a_little_more_complex.

Juel, Connie, and Diane Roper/Schneider. 1985. "The Influence of Basal Readers on First Grade Reading." *Reading Research Quarterly* 20 (2): 134–152.

Kamhi, Alan G., and Hugh W. Catts. 2012. *Language and Reading Disabilities* (3rd ed.). Boston: Allyn & Bacon.

Kessler, Brett, and Rebecca Treiman. 2001. "Relationships Between Sounds and Letters in English Monosyllables." *Journal of Memory and Language* 44 (4): 592–617. doi:10.1006/jmla.2000.2745.

Kilpatrick, David A. 2015. *Essentials of Assessing, Preventing, and Overcoming Reading Difficulties.* Hoboken, NJ: John Wiley and Sons.

———. 2016. *Equipped for Reading Success: A Comprehensive, Step-by-Step Program for Developing Phonemic Awareness and Fluent Word Recognition.* Syracuse, NY: Casey and Krisch.

———. 2020. "Game Changers: Research That Shaped the Science of Reading." *The Reading League Journal.* 1 (2): 13–14

Kintsch, Walter, and Eileen Kintsch. 2005. "Comprehension." In *Current Issues in Reading Comprehension and Assessment*, ed. S. G. Paris and S. A. Stahl (pp. 71–92). Mahwah, NJ: Lawrence Erlbaum.

Kirsch, Irwin, John de Jong, Dominique Lafontaine, Joy McQueen, Juliette Mendelovits, and Christian Monseur. 2002. *Reading for Change Performance and Engagement Across Countries. Results from Pisa 2000.* Organisation for Economic Co-operation and Development. https://www.oecd.org/edu/school/programmeforinternationalstudentassessmentpisa/33690904.pdf. Retrieved on March 20, 2020.

Kjeldsen, Ann-Christina, Antti Kärnä, Pekka Niemi, Åke Olofsson, and Katarina Witting. 2014. "Gains from Training in Phonological Awareness in Kindergarten Predict Comprehension in Grade 9. *Scientific Studies of Reading* 18 (6): 452-467. doi: 10.1080/10888438.2014.940080.

LaBerge, David, and S. Jay Samuels. 1974. "Toward a Theory of Automatic Information Processing in Reading." *Cognitive Psychology* 6 (2): 293–323. doi:10.1016/0010-0285(74)90015-2.

Layne, Steven L. 2015. *In Defense of Read-Aloud: Sustaining Best Practice.* Portland, ME: Stenhouse.

Lervåg, Arne, and Vibeke G. Aukrust. 2010. "Vocabulary Knowledge Is a Critical Determinant of the Difference in Reading Comprehension Growth Between First and Second Language Learners." *Journal of Child Psychology and Psychiatry* 51 (5): 612–620. doi:10.1111/j.14697610.2009.02185.x.

Lervåg, Arne, Charles Hulme, and Monica Melby-Lervåg. 2017. "Unpicking the Developmental Relationship Between Oral Language Skills and Reading Comprehension: It's Simple, but Complex." *Child Development* 89 (5): 1821–1838. doi:10.1111/cdev.12861.

Lever, Rosemary, and Monique Sénéchal. 2011. "Discussing Stories: On How a Dialogic Reading Intervention Improves Kindergartners' Oral Narrative Construction." *Journal of Experimental Child Psychology* 108 (1): 1–24. doi: 10.1016/j.jecp.2010.07.002.

Liben, David, and Meredith Liben. 2019. *Know Better, Do Better: Teaching the Foundation So Every Child Can Read.* West Palm Beach, FL: Learning Sciences International.

Liberman, Alvin M., Franklin S. Cooper, Donald P. Shankweiler, and Michael Studdert-Kennedy. 1967. "Perception of the Speech Code." *Psychological Review* 74 (6): 431–461. doi: 10.1037/h0020279.

Liberman, Isabelle Y., Donald P. Shankweiler, F. William Fischer, and Bonnie Carter. 1974. "Explicit Syllable and Phoneme Segmentation in the Young Child." *Journal of Experimental Child Psychology* 18 (2): 201–212. doi: 10.1016/0022-0965(74)90101-5.

Lobel, Arnold. 2003. *Frog and Toad Are Friends.* New York: HarperCollins.

Lundberg, Ingvar, Jørgen Frost, and Ole-Peter Petersen. 1988. "Effects of an Extensive Program for Stimulating Phonological Awareness in Preschool Children." *Reading Research Quarterly* 23 (3) 263–284. doi: 10.1598/RRQ.23.3.1.

McArthur, Genevieve, and Anne Castles. 2017. "Helping Children with Reading Difficulties: Some Things We Have Learned So Far." *Npj Science of Learning* 2 (1): Article 7. doi:10.1038/s41539-017-0008-3.

McCarthy, JoEllen. 2020. *Layers of Learning: Using Read-Alouds to Connect Literacy and Caring Conversations.* Portsmouth, NH. Stenhouse.

Melby-Lervåg, Monica, Solveig-Alma Halaas Lyster, and Charles Hulme. 2012. "Phonological Skills and Their Role in Learning to Read: A Meta-Analytic Review." *Psychological Bulletin* 138 (2): 322–352. doi: 10.1037/a0026744.

Mesmer, Heidi Anne E. 1999. "Scaffolding a Crucial Transition Using Text with Some Decodability." *Reading Teacher* 53 (2): 130–42. https://eric.ed.gov/?id=EJ594806.

———. 2019. *Letter Lessons and First Words: Phonics Foundations That Work.* Portsmouth, NH. Heinemann.

Mesmer, Heidi Anne E., James W. Cunningham, and Elfrieda H. Hiebert. 2012. "Toward a Theoretical Model of Text Complexity for the Early Grades: Learning from the Past, Anticipating the Future." *Reading Research Quarterly* 47 (3): 235–258.

Mesmer, Heidi Anne E., and Pricsilla L. Griffith. 2005. "Everybody's Selling It—But Just What Is Explicit, Systematic Phonics Instruction?" *Reading Teacher* 59 (4): 366–376.

Miller, Jan B. 1999. *The Effects of Training in Phonemic Awareness: A Meta-Analysis.* Ed.D. Diss. University of Kansas. https://kuscholarworks.ku.edu/bitstream/handle/1808/29864/miller_1999_2634649.pdf?sequence=1&isAllowed=y

Minor, Cornelius. 2018. *We Got This: Equity, Access, and the Quest to Be Who Our Students Need Us to Be.* Portsmouth, NH: Heinemann.

Moats, Louisa C., and Carol A. Tolman. 2019. *LETRS: Language Essentials for Teachers for Reading and Spelling,* 3rd ed. Dallas, TX: Voyager Sopris.

Montag, Jessica L., Michael N. Jones, and Linda B. Smith. 2015. "The Words Children Hear: Picture Books and the Statistics for Language Learning." *Psychological Science* 26 (9): 1489–1496. doi: 10.1177/0956797615594361.

Morais, José, Paul Bertelson, Luz Cary, and Jesus Alegria. 1986. "Literacy Training and Speech Segmentation." *Cognition* 24 (1–2): 45–64. doi: 10.1016/0010-0277(86)90004-1.

Morais, José, Luz Cary, Jesus Alegria, and Paul Bertelson. 1979. "Does Awareness of Speech as Sequence of Phonemes Arise Spontaneously?" *Cognition* 7 (4): 323–331. doi:10.1016/0010-0277(79)90020-9.

Morgan, Paul L., George Farkas, Marianne M. Hillemeir, and Steve Maczuga. 2017. "Replicated Evidence of Racial and Ethnic Disparities in Disability Identification in U.S. Schools." *Educational Researchers* 46 (6): 305-322. doi: 10.3102/0013189X17726282.

Nation, Kate, Paula Clarke, Catherine M. Marshall, and Marianne Durand. 2004. "Hidden Language Impairments in Children: Parallels Between Poor Reading Comprehension and Specific Language Impairments?" *Journal of Speech, Language and Hearing Research* 47 (1): 199–211. doi: 10.1044/1092-4388(2004/017).

Nation, Kate, Joanne Cocksey, Jo S. H. Taylor, and Dorothy V. M. Bishop. 2010. "A Longitudinal Investigation of Early Reading and Language Skills in Children with Poor Reading Comprehension." *Journal of Child Psychology and Psychiatry* 51 (9): 1031–1039. doi:10.1111/j.1469-7610.2010.02254.x.

National Early Literacy Panel (NELP). 2008. *Developing Early Literacy: Report of the National Early Literacy Panel.* Washington, DC: National Institute for Literacy.

National Institute of Child Health and Human Development. 2000. *Report of the National Reading Panel. Teaching Children to Read: An Evidence-Based Assessment of the Scientific Research Literature on Reading and Its Implications for Reading Instruction: Reports of the Subgroups* (NIH Publication No. 004754). Washington, DC: U.S. Government Printing Office.

Oakhill, Jane V., Kate Cain, and Peter E. Bryant. 2003. "The Dissociation of Word Reading and Text Comprehension: Evidence from Component Skills." *Language and Cognitive Processes* 18 (4): 443–468. doi:10.1080/09669760220114836.

Pearson, P. David, Nell K. Duke, Sonia Cabell, and Gwendolyn McMillon. 2020, October. *What Research Really Says About Teaching—And Why That Still Matters.* Presentation at International Literacy Association Annual Conference, New Orleans, LA, October 2020.

Perfetti, Charles A. 1985. *Reading Ability.* Oxford, UK. Oxford University Press.

———. 1991. "The Psychology, Pedagogy, and Politics of Teaching Reading." *Psychological Science* 2 (2): 70–76. doi: 10.1111/j.1467-9280.1991.tb00102.x.

———. 2007 "Reading Ability: Lexical Quality to Comprehension" *Scientific Studies of Reading* 11 (4): 257–357. doi: 10.1080/10888430701530730.

Perfetti, Charles A., and Lesley Hart. 2002. "The Lexical Quality Hypothesis." In *Precursors of Functional Literacy*, ed. L. Verhoeven, C. Elbr, and P. Reitsma (pp. 189–212). Amsterdam, The Netherlands: John Benjamins.

Perfetti, Charles A., N. Landi, and Jane Oakhill. 2005. "The Acquisition of Reading Comprehension Skill." In *The Science of Reading: A Handbook*, ed. M. J. Snowling and C. Hume (p. 227–247). Oxford, England: Blackwell.

Price-Mohr, Ruth, and Colin C. Price. 2020. "A Comparison of Children Aged 4–5 Years Learning to Read Through Instructional Texts Containing Either a High or a Low Proportion of Phonically Decodable Words." *Early Childhood Education* 48 (1): 39–47. doi: 10.1007/s10643-019-00970-4.

Quinn, Jamie M., Richard K. Wagner, Yaacov Petscher, and Danielle Lopez. 2015. "Developmental Relations Between Vocabulary Knowledge and Reading Comprehension: A Latent Change Score Modeling Study." *Child Development* 86(1): 159–175. doi:10.1111/cdev.12292.

Rect, Donna R., and Lauren Leslie. 1988. Effect of Prior Knowledge on Good and Poor Readers' Memory of Text. *Journal of Educational Psychology* 80 (1): 16-20. doi: 10.1037/0022-0663.80.1.16.

Reitsma, Pieter. 1983. "Printed Word Learning in Beginning Readers." *Journal of Experimental Child Psychology* 36 (2): 321–339. doi: 10.1016/0022-0965(83)90036-X.

Rose, Jim. 2006. *Independent Review of the Teaching of Early Reading Final Report.* U.K. Department for Education and Skills. http://dera.ioe.ac.uk/5551/2/report.pdf. Retrieved on May 17, 2020.

Rowe, Ken. 2005. "Teaching Reading: National Inquiry into the Teaching of Literacy. Department of Education, Science and Training, Australian Council for Educational Research." https://research.acer.edu.au/cgi/viewcontent.cgi?article=1004&context=tll_misc. Retrieved on April 4, 2020.

Sacks, David. 2003. *Language Visible: Unraveling the Mystery of the Alphabet from A to Z.* New York: Broadway Books.

Scarborough, Hollis S. 2001. "Connecting Early Language and Literacy to later Reading (Dis)abilities: Evidence, Theory, and Practice." In *Handbook for Research in Early Literacy*, ed. S. Neuman and D. Dickinson (pp. 97–110). New York: Guilford.

Schotter, Elizabeth, Klinton Bicknell, Ian Howard, Roger Levy, and Keith Rayner. 2014. "Task Effects Reveal Cognitive Flexibility Responding to Frequency and Predictability: Evidence from Eye Movements in Reading and Proofreading." *Cognition* 131 (1): 1–27. doi:10.1016/j.cognition.2013.11.018.

Seidenberg, Mark. 2013. "The Science of Reading and Its Educational Implications." *Language Learning and Development* 9 (4): 331–360. doi: 10.1080/15475441.2013.812017.

———. 2017. *Language at the Speed of Sight: How We Read, Why So Many Can't, and What Can Be Done About It.* New York: Hatchette Book Group.

Seidenberg, Mark, and James L. McClelland. 1989. "A Distributed, Developmental Model of Word Recognition and Naming." *Psychological Review* 97 (4): 523–568. doi: 10.1037//0033-295X.96.4.523.

Seymour, Philip H. K., Miko Aro, and James M. Erskine. 2003. "Foundation Literacy Acquisition in European Orthographies." *British Journal of Psychology* 94 (2): 143–174. doi:10.1348/000712603321661859.

Shanahan, Timothy. "Why Is It So Hard to Improve Reading Achievement?" *Shannahan on Literacy* (Blog). Jan. 25, 2020. https://shanahanonliteracy.com/blog/why-is-it-so-hard-to-improve-reading-achievement. Retrieved March 12, 2020.

Share, David L. 1995. "Phonological Recoding and Self-Teaching: Sine Qua Non of Reading Acquisition." *Cognition* 55 (2): 151–218. doi:10.1016/0010-0277(94)00645-2.

———. 1999. "Phonological Recoding and Orthographic Learning: A Direct Test of the Self-Teaching Hypothesis." *Journal of Experimental Child Psychology* 72 (2): 95–129. doi:10.1006/jecp.1998.2481.

———. 2004. "Orthographic Learning at a Glance: On the Time Course and Developmental Onset of Self-Teaching." *Journal of Experimental Child Psychology* 87 (4): 267–298. doi:10.1016/j.jecp.2004.01.001.

Snow, Catherine E., M. Susan Burns, and Peg Griffin. 1998. *Preventing Reading Difficulties in Young Children.* Washington, DC: National Academy Press.

Snow, Catherine E., and Connie Juel. 2005. "Teaching Children to Read: What Do We Know About How to Do It?" In *The Science of Reading: A Handbook*, ed. J. Snowling and C. Hulme (pp. 501–520). Malden, MA: Blackwell. doi:10.1002/9780470757642.ch26.

Solity, Jonathan, and Janet Vousden. 2009. "Real Books vs. Reading Schemes: A New Perspective from Instructional Psychology." *Educational Psychology* 29 (4): 469–511. doi:10.1080/01443410903103657.

Spencer, Llinos H., and John R. Hanley. 2004. "Learning a Transparent Orthography at Five Years Old: Reading Development of Children During Their First Year of Formal Reading Instruction in Wales." *Journal of Research in Reading* 27 (1): 1–14. doi:10.1111/j.1467-9817.2004.00210.x.

Stanovich, Keith E. 1986. "Matthew Effects in Reading: Some Consequences of Individual Differences in the Acquisition of Literacy." *Reading Research Quarterly* 21 (4): 360–407. Retrieved from http://www.jstor.org/stable/747612.

Stanovich, Keith E., and Richard. F. West. 1989. "Exposure to Print and Orthographic Processing." *Reading Research Quarterly* 24 (4): 402–433. doi:10.2307/747605.

Suggate, Sebastian P. 2016. "A Meta-Analysis of the Long-Term Effects of Phonemic Awareness, Phonics, Fluency, and Reading Comprehension Interventions." *Journal of Learning Disabilities* 49 (1): 77–96. https://epub.uni-regensburg.de/35639/1/0022219414528540.pdf.

Swanson, Elizabeth, Sharon Vaughn, Jeanne Wanzek, Yaacov Petscher, Jennifer Heckert, Christie Cavanaugh, Guliz Kraft, and Kathryn Tackett. 2011. "A Synthesis of Read-Aloud Interventions on Early Reading Outcomes Among Preschool Through Third Graders at Risk for Reading Difficulties." *Journal of Learning Disabilities* 44 (3): 258–275. doi: 10.1177/0022219410378444.

Tik, Martin, Ronald Sladky, Caroline Di Bernardi Luft, David Willinger, André Hoffmann, Michael J. Banissy, Joydeep Bhattacharya, and Christian Windischberger. 2018. "Ultra-High-Field fMRI Insights on Insight: Neural Correlates of the Aha! Moment." *Human Brain Mapping* 39 (8): 3241–3252. doi: 10.1002/hbm.24073.

Torgesen, Joseph K. 2002. "The Prevention of Reading Difficulties." *Journal of School Psychology.* 40 (1): 7–26. doi: 10.1016/S0022-4405(01)00092-9.

Treiman, Rebecca, and Brett Kessler. 2014. *How Children Learn to Write Words.* Oxford, England: Oxford University Press.

Tunmer, William E., and James W. Chapman. 2012. "Does Set for Variability Mediate the Influence of Vocabulary Knowledge on the Development of Word Recognition Skills?" *Scientific Studies of Reading* 16: 122–140. doi:10.1080/10888438.2010.542527.

Turkeltaub, Peter E., Lynn Gareau, Donna L. Flowers, Thomas A. Zeffiro, and Guinevere F. Eden. 2003. "Development of Neural Mechanisms for Reading." *Nature Neuroscience* 7 (8): 767–773. doi: 10.1038/nn1065.

Wagner, Richard K., and Joseph K. Torgesen. 1987. "The Nature of Phonological Processing and Its Causal Role in the Acquisition of Reading Skills." *Psychological Bulletin* 101 (2): 192–212. doi:10.1037/00332909.101.2.192.

Weekes, Brendan S. 1997. "Differential Effects of Number of Letters on Word and Nonword Naming Latency." *The Quarterly Journal of Experimental Psychology* 50 (2): 439–456. doi:10.1080/713755710.

Whitehurst, Grover, Francine L. Falco, Christopher J. Lonigan, Janet E. Fischel, Barbara D. DeBaryshe, Marta C. Valdez-Menchaca, and Marie B. Caulfield. 1988. "Accelerating Language Development Through Picture Book Reading." *Developmental Psychology* 24 (4): 552–559. doi: 10.1037/0012-1649.24.4.552.

Willingham, Daniel T. 2017. *The Reading Mind: A Cognitive Approach to Understanding How the Mind Reads.* San Francisco, CA: Jossey-Bass.

Wolf, Maryanne. 2007. *Proust and the Squid: The Story and Science of the Reading Brain.* New York. Harper Perennial.

Yates, Kari. 2015. *Simple Starts: Making the Move to a Reader-Centered Classroom.* Portsmouth, NH: Heinemann.

Yates, Kari, and Christina Nosek. 2018. *To Know and Nurture a Reader: Conferring with Confidence and Joy.* Portsmouth, NH: Stenhouse.

Ziegler, Johannes, Conrad Perry, and Marco Zorzi. 2014. "Modeling Reading Development Through Phonological Decoding and Self-Teaching: Implications for Dyslexia." *Philosophical Transactions of the Royal Society B: Biological Sciences* 369: Article 20120937. doi:10.1098/rstb.2012.0397.

INDEX

t = table
f = figure

175

meaning processing system, 13–14, 15t, 16, 17t, 22, 27, 28, 38, 65, 75, 99, 103, 112, 113, 121, 124t, 127

Melby-Lervåg, Monica, 11, 17, 38, 43

Mesmer, Heidi, 67, 94

Miller, Jan, 38, 41

Minor, Cornelius, 2

mirror invariance, reading and, 66

Moats, Louisa, 36, 53, 54, 67, 93, 119, 139, 144

Montag, Jessica, 28

Morais, José, 37

Morgan, Paul, 1

MSV model, 111–115, 117, 118, 121,
  Four-Part Processing model and, 112
  traditional use of, 113t–114t
  V→MS, 117, 118f, 124, 125f, 129f, 130

Multisensory scaffolds, 50

N

Nation, Kate, 11, 20, 21, 41, 93, 98

National Early Literacy Panel, 40

National Institute of Child Health and Human Development, 40, 42, 74

Natural, 14, 30, 36, 37

Nosek, Christina, 156

novelty, repetition versus, 140–142, 150t, 152t, 158

O

Oakhill, Jane, 42

oral language 17, 18, 21–23, 29, 36, 38, 133, 135, 143, 144, 147, 149, 154, 155, 157, 168

109 high-frequency words, 92, 101

oral language comprehension, development, 17, 18, 21–22, 23, 144, 147

high-leverage instructional routines and, 24–26

read-aloud texts and, 24, 28–29

repeating, expanding and, 29

text sets and, 24

orthographic knowledge, 27, 66, 67–68, 70, 72, 81, 94, 106, 116, 119, 123t–124t, 154
  assessment, 84, 85t

orthographic frustration, 146, 147

orthographic learning, 146, 147, 148, 149t, 157

orthographic mapping, 95–96, 97, 99, 101, 103–105, 108, 127–128, 145, 151, 153
  defined, 103, 137
  examples, 96t
  routine, 104t

orthographic processing system, 17–18, 22, 65, 75, 112t, 113, 121

orthographic value, sense-making value versus, 140–141, 142t, 150, 152t

orthography, 70

deep or shallow, 70, 72, 75, 95, 146

Ouellette, Gene, 42, 91, 94

P

parenthetical explanation, 28

patterned texts, 137, 138–139, 140, 141, 143, 144, 149t, 150, 152–153, 157

Perfetti, Charles, 42, 98, 116, 119, 127

Petersen, Ole-Peter, 40

phon
  defined, 38
  instruction, 39t

phonemes, 36, 39t, 54t, 55t, 56, 57–58, 70, 95, 104t